THE VOICE

THE UNPARALLELED LIFE OF

ROGER HUSTON

BY VICTORIA M. HOWARD

AuthorHouse™
1663 Liberty Drive
Bloomington, IN 47403
www.authorhouse.com
Phone: 1 (800) 839-8640

Published by AuthorHouse 04/15/2019

ISBN: 978-1-7283-0655-1 (sc)
ISBN: 978-1-7283-0657-5 (hc)
ISBN: 978-1-7283-0656-8 (e)

Library of Congress Control Number: 2019903973

Permission was granted for use of photos used of any living person

Print information available on the last page.

This book is printed on acid-free paper.

authorHOUSE®

Dedication

When you devote your life to your career, in my case Harness Racing, something must get put on the back burner.

From 1960 to the present, my career as a race announcer always came first. Unfortunately, it was my family who suffered the most. My duty and responsibility of announcing races at fairs, racetracks, or other venues were put ahead of my loved ones.

Even the calculated birthdate of my daughter Nevele who was born by caesarian on September 16, 1983 was pre-arranged so I could leave the following day to call races in Delaware, Ohio, at The Little Brown Jug.

Throughout the years I have missed eventful birthdays, weddings and even the birth of my precious granddaughter Kinsley, because of my obligation to The Columbiana County Fair in Lisbon, Ohio.

Although my wife couldn't understand the unconditional commitment I had to my career, my daughter Nevele always did. (And yes, she was named after my favorite horse—NEVELE PRIDE)

So it is my honor to dedicate this book to the love of my life, my daughter Nevele, who is my pride and joy. Fortunately for me she is far more loving and better mannered than her notorious namesake.

Roger

Preface

As I sit here recollecting the events that have made what I consider to be a stimulating, unique and blessed life, my eyes begin to tear for many of the people I will be talking about are no longer with us.

My parents, who were my biggest fans are gone, but will always live in my heart, along with many other family members.

A dear friend, Sam McKee, one of the best race announcers ever and who I considered 'a son' died in 2017 at the young age of 54.

Although these people are no longer with me they will always be kept alive in my heart and through the pages of this book.

Yes, I've met a lot of interesting people in my life and believe everyone has a best-selling story to tell. I believe I do, too. It's not that I'm special; but God has blessed me with a career I not only lived and breathed for sixty years but opened doors to opportunities that were beyond any wild dreams I ever imagined. In my eyes, I have never worked one day in my life.

For years many people have asked me why I've never written a book. I'm not a celebrity or politician but have been an integral part of what I consider one of the greatest sports in the world: Harness Racing.

For over half a century I've been involved in different aspects of the industry: handicapping, training, owning, driving and announcing races.

I've called and witnessed some of the very best horseraces; from the thrill of setting world records to the heartache of a heavy favorite break stride, or worse, involved in an accident.

I've called races at fairs and racetracks across North America and overseas. Throughout the years I met and befriended top trainers, owners, drivers; even caretakers who have meant as much to me as the most influential people in the business. Some of these people are still with us; while others I'm certain are up there working with a horse in some way.

When my son-in-law Dustin asked me to write a book about my adventures and career, I called a woman I've known for forty years who has written many books and who I consider to be a very good friend, Victoria Howard– but she's Vicki to me.

Unfortunately Vicki lives 2,000 miles away so collaborating is going to be a challenge for us; but being that we are both Virgo's, we thrive on challenges.

While writing this book many memories re-surfaced which were buried in the back of my mind. Even though some may be pensive for the person has since passed, they were still important times in my life so I wanted to share them with you. I hope to make you feel as if you were there with me, experiencing the thrills and ups and downs I have encountered in my career of Harness Racing.

Roger

Acknowledgements

First and foremost I would like to thank my family for understanding and condoning my absences at many important occasions, due to my obligation of calling races. You are the ones who encouraged me to write this book after years of tossing the idea around.

To my friend and author Vicki Howard, for making my dream a reality, by putting my life on paper and creating a book that will be my family's legacy.

To all the people in the book-- those who are alive and those deceased, for without you there would be no book.

Thanks to all who gave permission to use their pictures for the book.

To the U.S.T.A. for helping find and allowing the use of certain horse photos.

To Kelly Spencer, for taking the wonderful photo used on the front cover.

And to all the horses, each and every one, that I had the pleasure of calling in a race. No matter who you were: whether you were a cheap claimer or a World Champion, you were all significant and special to me.

Table of Contents

A Word From The Author

I have personally known Roger Huston for forty years. The very first time I heard that unique compelling intonation was the day Roger announced my Standardbred, Who Du Girl, winning her first race at The Meadows Racetrack----which was also my initial win as an owner/trainer.

Although Who Du was merely a $2,500 claimer (but in my eyes she was a champion) Roger made the race sound like she had just won The Little Brown Jug. Sixty years later, Huston is still calling every race, no matter what class it is, as if it were a million dollar race.

That was it! I was hooked-- line and sinker-- and decades later I am still involved in this exhilarating, yet at times nerve-wracking sport.

At that time Roger had relocated to Pennsylvania from Florida where he had been calling the horseraces at Pompano Park Racetrack, known as 'The Winter Capital of Harness Racing'.

In 1976 Huston arrived at The Meadows Racetrack located in Washington, Pennsylvania and has been a permanent fixture ever since. For the past forty-four years he has been calling the races there, including the legendary Adios Race. (Heck, that's twice as long than most marriages last!)

In his career Roger has called more than 178,000 races; covering at least 144 tracks in 19 states and 8 countries throughout his career.

Sports in the United States are an important part of American culture. Competition in sports has been prominent since the ancient Greeks invented the Olympics, just as horseracing has been around since the days of Ben-Hur and the chariot races. (Which was the most popular sport spectacle of the Roman and Byzantine Eras.)

Thus, there has always been a need for someone to vocally describe what is happening on the field of play. This is where sport announcers are needed.

As far as Superstar Sport announcers, Vin Scully has long been considered the best in baseball, former player Pat Summerall and partner John Madden is the pinnacle in football, and who could forget the instantly recognizable voice of the inimitable sports journalist Howard Cosell?

In Harness Racing several names come to mind such as Carl Becker and Frank Salive, but perhaps none has matched the all-encompassing legend of harness racings' Roger Huston.

Besides calling horseraces Roger also finds time to dab in other avenues and provides audio for local merchant commercials. In fact, Roger and I once filmed several television commercials promoting The John Howard Automobile Dealerships in the nineties.

It doesn't matter where you are, when you hear 'that voice' you instantly know a trotting or pacing race is imminent.

Roger's signature tone has been compared to the unmistakable voice of sports announcer Howard Cosell who was famous for saying, *"This is Howard Cosell on Sports."*

At first Cosell's predominant style was unabashed adulation, offering a brassy counterpoint that was first ridiculed then copied until it became the dominant note of sports broadcasting.

Although there are many good announcers in Harness Racing there is only one undistinguishable voice--- and that is Huston's. So the day Roger called and asked my thoughts about writing his autobiography, it was a no-brainer. The only thing I muttered was, *"Why did it take 50 years for it to happen?"*

But in life everything is timing and this is the time to write the life story of a talented, amazing, one-of-a-kind man who I am proud to call my good friend.

As a writer I have heard some unconventional stories, but I don't know anyone else who has worked harder, been unconditionally devoted and brought more excitement and joy to people worldwide than Roger Huston.

Although I have co-written several books on Harness Racing, this book is different because not only is it an autobiography of a unique man's life, but also an informative book about the greatest horses, races and people in what I also consider the best sport on this planet—Harness Racing.

It is my honor to put on paper the crazy, exhilarant adventures of the one and only, 'The Voice'—Roger Huston. I hope to do Roger and his story justice and bring a smidgen of excitement that he has brought to millions of people worldwide.

Victoria M Howard

THE LITTLE BROWN JUG
DELAWARE, OHIO

"If you've never been on your feet, you better get up now!"

It's 1985, Little Brown Jug Day and *Falcon Seelster* with driver Tom Harmer just passed the 3/4 pole in a then unheard time of 1:22.4 as race caller Roger Huston sensing a world record was imminent, implored the huge crowd to get in view positioning NOW!

    As the horses get in behind the gate, Roger Huston announces.......

"The invitational Pace. The gate swings around the turn and heeeeere they come!.........

    They're off and pacing. Going for the lead is Falcon Seelster in the middle of the track........ Past the quarter in a speedy 27 seconds.

    They reach the half in 54. 3!!! 27. 3 second quarter.

    What's the ¾'s gonna be? 1:22.4!!!

    And Falcon Seelster opens up for Tom Harmer! If you've never been on you're feet, you better get up now!

    It's Falcon Seelster opening up now by 15 lengths, 17, 19. Falcon Seelster and Tom Harmer--- LOOK AT THE TIMER! 1:51!!!!!!!!!!"

That history-making race took place on Jug Day in 1985.

Thirty-Four years after *Falcon Seelster* was victorious in World Record Time, Roger Huston can still be heard calling the upsets and favorites of Harness Racing every year at The Little Brown Jug—but that's another chapter later on in the book.

Calling that momentous race was "Just another ordinary day at the office" for Roger Huston, race caller extraordinaire, who literally makes even the most inconsequential trotting or pacing race sound like the most exciting event you've ever witnessed.

For most people, watching a horserace accurately each time is probably a pipedream, but for Roger Huston, also known as **THE VOICE,** it was merely routine; and like the great athletes he described in action, he made it look and sound easy and "Did it his way."

Present Day
2018

As I sit in my office reminiscing and relating memories and special life experiences to Vicki Howard, I can't help but get choked up. I'm 76-years old and not only the father to two daughters, Cami Sue and Nevele, stepson Troy and step-grandson Tyler; but God has blessed my family with two beautiful granddaughters, Regan and Kinsley. I live from day-to-day, for after all 76 is on the downslide.

2018 was another great year in Harness Racing. World Records have been broke and the races seem to go faster and faster. This years' Adios was won by *Dorsoduro Hanover* in the time of 1:50.1, and *Courtly Choice* was victorious in The Little Brown Jug in 1:49.4.

Unreal, for I remember the time if you had a 2:00 trotter you had a great one. Today trotters are going in 1:48.4, (*Homicide Hunter*) and a filly named *Atlanta* did the impossible and won The 2018 Hambletonian, beating out a field of the nation's best trotting colts. After an owner's dispute, *Atlanta* was put online to buy out partner/trainer Rick Zeron's 5%. The sale closed at a whopping $1,550,000! It was the highest price ever paid for a Standardbred.

Some say Harness Racing is dying and in many ways it is, but for myself and die-hard fans it will never die! The horses are being bred better and the races are going faster.

Today, women trainers are not only giving the male trainers a run for their money, (Casie Coleman, Linda Toscano, Julie Miller, Nancy Takter Johansson, Jacqueline Ingrassia and Riina Rekila) but are soaring ahead! So you can no longer say Harness Racing is a man's game. In 2018 a pacing stallion named *Captain Treacherous* sent his first crop racing, with sons *Captain Crunch* and *Captain Ahab* dominating the stake races.

McWicked, the son of *McArdle* was a champion at 3 but then became lost in the shuffle for several years. He resurrected at age 7 and was hard to beat, ranking #1 in the sport's year-end poll. Although *McWicked* was a big disappointment at ages 4, 5 and 6, the bay gelding showed his fans and competition that "It's not over 'til it's over," and proved to the youngsters that age is irrelevant. In 2018 he won 'Aged Pacer and Horse of the Year'.

Local owned *Foiled Again* beat the odds and raced up until he was no longer permitted to race (age 14). On December 31, 2018 *Foiled Again*, the richest harness horse ever, made his final start in front of thousands of adoring fans at his home track, The Meadows. I was so honored to call this superstar's last race. After a career consisting of 331 starts: 109 victories, 70 seconds and 46 thirds and raking over $7.6 million, this superstars' shoes were pulled in the winners' circle and he is now enjoying a well-deserved retirement in the green grass. I think it will be some time before his money earning record is surpassed.

On February 24, 2019, *Foiled Again* made a personal surprise guest appearance at The Dan Patch Awards for winning The Stanley Bergstein Proximity Award.

And one of harness racing's greatest trainers, Hall of Famer Jimmy Takter, surprised racing fans when he announced he decided to retire from Harness Racing. Having another phenomenal year with horses *Tactical Landing* and *Manchego,* they added to the long list of many Takter Stars: *Kadabra, Gleam, Always B Miki, Money Maker* and the list goes on. Yes, 2018 was a very good year!

Before I start talking about the great horses and big races I've called in my career, since this is my life story I'm going to start out with my childhood. I hope I don't bore you too much, but if I do I promise it will get more exciting!

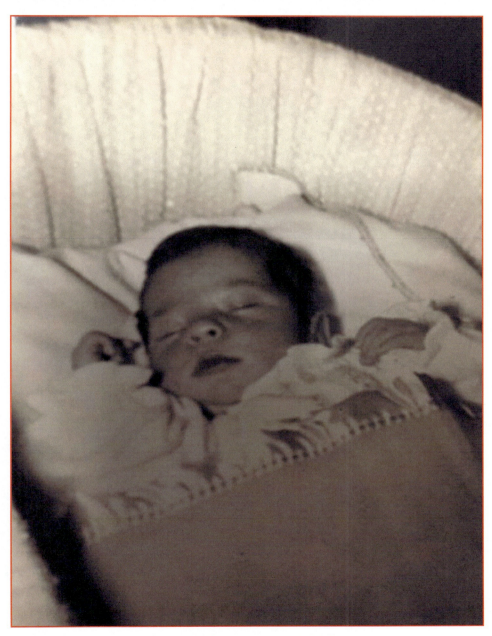

My baby picture 1942

Me and my sister Joyce

My parents, Cecil and Irene Huston, on their Wedding Day

The naming of The Roger Huston Announcers Booth, with Jason Settlemoir, Tom Wright, Susie Dupler-Telle and Daughter Nevele.
The 50ᵗʰ Little Brown Jug in 2017

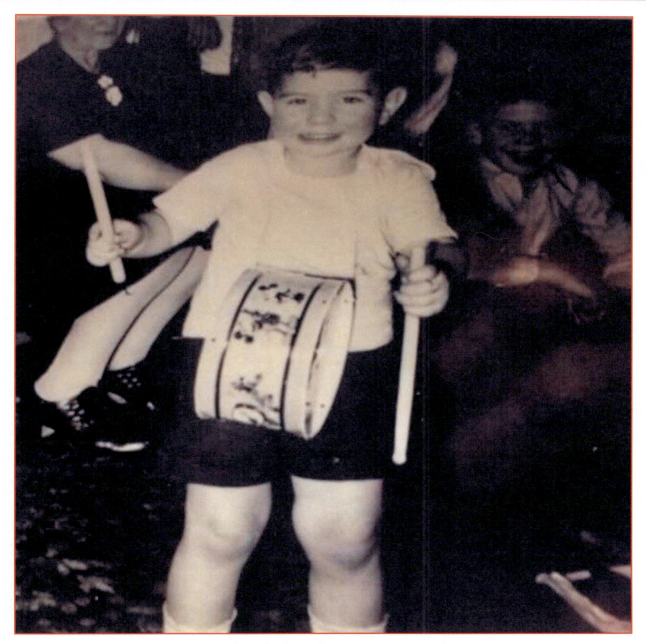

Roger, The Little Drummer Boy

Greene County Marker

CHAPTER ONE

It All Started In Xenia, Ohio

THE BEGINNING OF A REAL-LIFE FAIRYTALE

Every fairytale has a magical beginning and in the case of Roger Huston, it was no different. It is said that the good Lord bestows a special talent on each and every one of us. Some are born with exquisite beauty; others artistic talent or music ability, and some people are blessed with a brilliant mind.

In 1452, in the Tuscany region a baby boy would grow up to be an Italian painter, sculptor, architect and inventor. His name was Leonardo da Vinci / aka The Italian Renaissance man.

On January 4, 1643, a boy was born in London named (Sir) Isaac Newton. He grew up to be a physicist who would develop the principles of modern physics, including the laws of the motion.

On January 8, 1935, in Tupelo, Mississippi, The King of Rock and Roll –Elvis Aaron Presley--- rocked his way into the world. Elvis would become known as a film and music icon that drove women wild with his signature 'Hip Shakes and Gyrates'.

On February 27, 1932, in Hampstead, London, England, a girl named Elizabeth Rosemond Taylor was born who would be known as, "The most beautiful woman in the world". Every man lusted after the violet-eyed, raven-haired beauty and every woman wanted to be her.

Ten years later on a balmy September 16, 1942, in a city called Xenia, Ohio, (pronounced /zeen-ya) a son was born to Cecil and Stella Irene Huston named Roger Eugene who would grow up to be known as "The Voice." Throughout his career Huston would call more horseraces than any other announcer in history. (And is still going on)

MY FAMILY TREE

As far as my lineage, I asked my grandfather Ross Huston what nationality we were and he matter-of-factly replied, "Buckeyes." For those of you who have never heard of a "Buckeye," it's a nickname for residents of Ohio—the Buckeye State.

My grandmother was a Gardner whose family tree was traced to a man named Henry Tiffin. Henry was the first Governor of Ohio in (I believe) 1803. I don't know for certain but we guessed our ancestry to be English and Scottish.

I made my debut into the world in a place called Xenia. It is a quiet city in Ohio that has a history of severe storm activity. According to local legend the Shawnee Indians referred to that area as "The place of the devil wind" or "The land of the crazy winds." So it was no surprise that the day I was born Dr. Rayburn McClelland asked the attending nurse if there was a racetrack nearby for it seemed someone in the room---most likely me--- was heard to bellow out, "*WAGER NOWWWW!*"

As Dr. McClelland stared in disbelief he told my mother, "*Ma'am you're baby has an incredible set of lungs! I bet someday he will be a radio show host, auctioneer, or perhaps a race announcer!*"

(Perhaps that is why Huston would grow up to become one of the most renowned and instantly recognizable voices in the world of Harness Racing?)

THE GLORIOUS 40s

My dad was a hard worker who always provided well for his family. He started out working as a milk deliveryman and also drove the city bus before eventually going to work on a farm for his Uncle Ert Huston.

In 1945-1946 dad took a job as manager at the Shoemake Dairy Farm, located in Alpha, Ohio. There he raised crops such as wheat and corn and milked 75 guernseys a day.

The milk was shipped to Dayton, Ohio where it was bottled, being that Shoemake was the only dairy farm supplier in the area. The dairy business was good and by 1952 the number of guernseys increased 60% to 125. That was a lot of milking!

My father hired a man named Ted Ater to run the combine. I often got to ride with Ted and occasionally he would let me steer. One day Ted's help didn't show up for work so he asked if I could steer the truck between the two gates.

He placed a stone on the gas pedal allowing the truck to creep 4 to 5 miles per hour. Ted told me once I got the vehicle between the gates to kick the stone away, which would stop it.

Being a young boy my feet didn't reach the pedal so I had to stand up and stretch my leg out.

I did exactly what he said and all went well, but when we reached the barn my mother was waiting there, arms crossed and screaming at Ted for allowing me to drive, for I was only five-years-old!

But Ted said to *"Be there,"* and there I was!

****

We were a very close family, so when my granddad, Stanley Matthews' (on mothers' side) health began to fail, he came to live with us.

Our house was plenty large enough to accompany another person, so my parents converted our dining room into a bedroom for him.

I remember granddad and I spending a lot of time together. These were great memories, for we always had fun.

One winter day during one of our many walks we went to the cow barn. The cement floor was cold, dirty and soiled by the guernseys waste.

Granddad looked at me and said, *"Butch, don't ever drink beer!"* (Butch was the nickname he gave me)

I thought that was a strange thing to tell a young boy and asked him, *"Why?"*

He looked at me with a serious look on his face and said, *"Don't you know what beer is made of? It's cow piss and sawdust!"*

I guess that's one reason I never liked drinking the brew!

My granddad was quite a character. The memories of him are warm and loving, except for one: the day he passed on. It was probably the most traumatic thing I went through as a child, and one I will never forget.

I woke early one morning as I heard a car pull up in front of our house. I looked out of the upstairs window and saw a long dark vehicle I'd never seen before pull into the driveway. My dad let two strange men inside as I heard mom crying.

The men walked into granddads room wheeling a stretcher. Not exactly knowing what was happening I watched as granddads covered body was placed inside the ambulance.

Although I dearly miss him, I know one day I will see him again.

****

One of the things I still look forward to is summertime, for that's when I make my rounds to the county fairs to call horseraces.

I guess one reason it's so special is because as far back as I can remember I'd accompany my parents to the Greene County Fair in Xenia to watch the horseraces.

I'd listen to the announcer as he called the races and tried my hardest to memorize all the horse's names. I was in awe watching these large, four-legged athletes hooked to a sulky go in a circle at a fast speed.

When we got home I would take out my tricycle and pedal around the house trying to reduplicate the race I had just watched, but my tricycle wasn't sufficient so eventually I designed my own sulky.

Young children have wild imaginations and mine was no different. In our house we had an overstuffed chair, so I placed the pullout section for the dinner table on top of the chairs' arms to make a seat and attached two belts to a kitchen chair that served as driving lines.

I went out to our yard and broke off a branch from a weeping willow tree that acted as a whip and imitated a driver steering a horse in a race.

(Of course I wouldn't actually hit the horse, for I could never hurt an animal, so I hit the shaft.)

Little did I know that seventy-years later I would be getting paid for doing what I consider to be "The best job in the world!"

****

As a young boy my parents instilled in me a good work ethic; saying anything I wanted I had to work for. As a youngster I helped my grandfather Ross Huston mow lawns in Xenia. I also had a paper route with over 100 customers for the six-day-a- week delivery.

My paper route was from The Xenia Field House to Greene Memorial Hospital. The area was developed in the early 50s so when we moved from the farm we built a house in that section of Xenia.

I was a firm believer in putting the newspaper inside the screen door, so my customers would always have a dry paper and wouldn't have to trek out to the yard to get it. This kind gesture really paid off with good tips--- especially at Christmas.

One year I was a bit obstinate and let my temper get in the way as one of my customers failed to give me anything for Christmas, so I started wrapping his paper and tossing it on the front porch.

Well that act of rebellion came back to bite me in my behind because one of those times the paper broke the glass in the man's storm door. That was a hard and costly lesson, for the price to replace the glass cost me two or three weeks of my hard earned money!

But overall, it was a very good time for many of those customers became lifelong friends and remained so until I moved away in 1967.

****

My next job was at The James Super Value Grocery Store.

There was a man named Butch Green who drove the Johnson Cab in Xenia. Butch would pick up shoppers after they were done shopping and drive them home with their groceries.

Even as a young boy my mind was always thinking of different ways I could earn some extra money; so I worked out a 'deal' with Butch where I would phone him when someone needed a ride and in return, he was to pay me a quarter for every customer I got him. Well, I got Butch a lot of fares but he never paid me a cent.

Thinking back now I imagine if I got half the money Butch owed me, I could have bought myself a nice horse or maybe that motorcycle I always wanted!

THE NIFTY 50s

Children inherit personality and hereditary traits from their parents or family members. I guess you could say that I inherited my talent as an announcer from Uncle Don.

In 1953 Uncle Don started announcing horseraces at The Allentown and York Fair in Pennsylvania.

Steve Phillips, the brilliant man who invented The Mobile Starting Gate, got Uncle Don the job. (See pg. 20) Uncle Don was so good at calling races; eventually he went on to call the races at Lebanon Raceway.

At the time I was eleven-years-old and would accompany my uncle three to five nights a week to the races. I remember riding with him in his car while he puffed on cheap stogies; gagging from the smoke but thrilled to be there, so I kept my mouth shut.

When I was thirteen-years-old, Uncle Don and I went to Miami County Fair in Troy, Ohio, for he was to call the races. I kept looking at the clock as the time ticked by, afraid we would be late; but Uncle Don told me not to worry for we had plenty of time. Well wouldn't you know it but on the way to the fair we had a flat tire and had to stop and change it. By the time we pulled into the track The National Anthem was playing, so being strapped for time Uncle Don asked me to park the car.

I watched as he ran like a bat out of hell to the judges' stand. That incident is most likely the reason I always arrive at the races two hours early.

****

I was always taught, "To be the best you can at whatever you do and never ever look down on yourself." How you see yourself is how people will see you and how they will treat you. See yourself as the WINNER you are, no matter what, and a WINNER you will always be!

A good teacher can inspire hope, ignite the imagination and instill a love of learning, and Uncle Don was the best teacher anyone could hope for. I owe him a lot and hope and pray he realized how much he meant to me.

As far as school goes, I was a good student. I received good grades without having to exert too much of my time; thus my parents allowed me to dabble in my hobby, which was attending the races and practice my race calling.

One day Uncle Don took the plunge and purchased a filly named *Ginger D Direct* who was by the great sire *Billy Direct*.

Like many boys I wanted a motorcycle, but of course like most parents they wouldn't allow it, so I began hanging around the barn jogging Uncle Don's filly and discovered I really enjoyed it.

There was a horseman named Johnny Bush who owned a fifteen-year-old mare named *Emily Martin* who he had retired. Poor *Emily* was always a bridesmaid—never a bride. She never won a race in her entire racing career, but placed many times.

From the money I made working at the grocery store (no thanks to Butch Green) I saved a substantial amount. Instead of buying that motorcycle I always wanted, I bought *Emily* from Johnny and began training her. I would pretend we were racing in the Hambletonian. (Of course, we always won!) In our world, Emily never lost a race. I even went as far as to pretend she got her picture taken in the winners' circle. Hopefully, it made her feel like she was a winner!

Not long after we bought *Emily* we decided to breed her to a sire named *Waybloom* by *Dean Hanover.* Her first foal, a filly, was on the small side so I named her *Midgeway,* who we eventually sold.

I learned a lot from working with *Emily* and she will always hold a spot in my heart for she was the one horse that really got me involved in the wonderful world of Harness Racing.

****

Wherever there are horseraces, there is gambling. Although I'm not the gambling type I have to give credit to my dabbling now and then in betting horses to a man named Herman Scott.

Herman owned a trotter named *Wampum.* Many times when *Wampum* was in to race, Herman would tell me, *"I think my horse has a shot tonight, Butch. Maybe you should throw a few bucks on him."*

Of course I wasn't old enough to bet, so Darbyshire a real estate insurance agent, would buy the tickets for me. Well more times than not *Wampun* won.

When Darbyshire would hand me my winning money I thought, *"This is easy."*

Little did I know how hard it really is to pick a winner!

Steve Phillips -- The Inventor of the Original Starting Gate

Uncle Don at Lebanon Raceway

CHAPTER TWO

The Beginning of A Lifelong Career

THE SWINGING 60s

My career as a race announcer could have been over before it ever got started if my cousin Olive had anything to do with it. In 1960 I was a senior at Xenia High School and cousin Olive taught a speech class there. She wanted me to enroll in her class, but I felt it wouldn't be a good idea because we would most likely butt heads, so I declined.

At the time I was the P.A. Announcer for the high school team, The Buccaneers. When I refused to take my cousins' class she got mad and went to the school board, asking them to pass a motion that the P.A. Announcers had to be members of her class. Once again, Uncle Don came to the rescue and helped me get out of it.

Uncle Don had taken a job at a new local radio station, WHBM-FM 103.9 as Sports Director. The station was in the need of other employees, so he recommended me for a part-time job spinning records that eventually led to my becoming News Director. I also worked with my Uncle doing play-by-play football, basketball and Babe Ruth baseball. At that time I was a senior working forty hours a week-- after school and weekends.

In the early 60s the radio station became involved with WHIO Radio in Dayton (along with The Dayton Power and Light Company) in a15-minute news broadcast.

I was a co-anchor, along with Phil Donahue. Yes, 'the' Phil Donahue who was also starting his radio career before he went on to television. Eventually, Phil became an American media personality, writer, film producer and creator of The Phil Donahue Show that ran for 29 years. He also married beautiful actress Marlo Thomas, the daughter of Danny Thomas.

When Winston Haner, a talk show host on WHIO who did the afternoon segment decided to retire, they asked Phil and me if one of us wanted the job. At the time I was going to Wilmington College and unable to take it, so Phil took the opportunity that led to a brilliant career in broadcasting.

I often wonder if I had accepted the job would the same thing have happened to me? I mean---Can you see it? The Roger Huston Show! (Just kidding!)

But if I had taken that job I wouldn't have the life that I do now. And I'm a believer that nothing in life happens by coincidence and everything that happens is *supposed* to happen, so I have thankfully embraced the blessed life I was given and wouldn't change it for anything.

****

Doing play-by-play football and basketball was a huge thrill. The station couldn't afford to pay two guys for each game, so when we had double-headers, Uncle Don would do the prime time game and I would do the other. Talk about announcer bloopers!

One time Uncle Don and I were doing a Central State University football game when the quarterback dropped back into the end zone to throw a pass and got sacked. In describing the action Don said, *"Oh, they nailed him to the cross!"*

I had a similar instance when calling a race in Australia in the 90s at Adelaide Raceway. Back then most tracks had a hub rail and one of my favorite sayings was, "*So and so is nailed to the rail.*" The only problem was this particular time the horse's name was *Messiah!*

Getting back to my early days…. I distinctly remember one Sunday in April or May of 1960 when Uncle Don was set to call the matinee races in Wilmington, Ohio. He asked if I wanted to accompany him and of course I jumped at the chance.

After he called the first race he paged me and asked if I would announce Post Parade in the second, as he had to excuse himself, for Mother Nature was calling.

He said he'd be right back and assured me I would do just fine. After the Post Parade was called and there was no Uncle Don, I started to panic.

Bobby Williams, the presiding judge at the time informed me, "*Don's not coming back, Roger. You're on your own!*'

I was shaking so bad I could hardly hold the microphone. Thus my debut as a race announcer was horrible, but by the seventh race I had settled down a bit and managed to finish calling the race card.

***

After graduating from high school I enrolled in Wilmington College, which was located 18 miles from Xenia. At the time I wanted to be a schoolteacher; with plans of teaching nine months a year and announcing races in the summertime.

During the first semester I learned a lot about speaking from a Professor named Hugh Heiland. At that time Hugh hosted a weekly radio show on Harness Racing.

Hugh was a well-liked man who knew a lot of influential people. We've remained friends throughout the years and in 2000 when I was inducted to The Little Brown Jug 'Wall of Fame' Hugh showed up to honor me. His passing was a heartfelt loss as he was instrumental in my life as an announcer.

In my senior year I lacked four hours to graduate. I had been so busy getting my career as an announcer started I ignored the fact that graduation day was nearing and I was four hours shy.

My advisor, Elizabeth Kinzig, was very upset that I didn't get my degree so she offered to help and pulled some strings.

She petitioned the Board of Academic Affairs to allow the hours in Biology to count towards my minor and take four hours of special instruction from her. In return, I would get my diploma.

Ms. Kinzig asked me to type a paper on, "The Advantages and Disadvantages of Educational TV in the Beavercreek School System."

I remember exactly when I wrote the story for it was on the historic night that astronaut Neil Armstrong stepped on the moon. ("That's one small step for man, one giant leap for mankind.") I was staying at the Curtiss Hotel in Mt. Vernon, Ohio for I was there to call races at the Knox County Fair.

During those years at Wilmington I became Sports Information Director and P.A. Announcer for football and basketball games. My last two years I also served as SID for the Mid-Ohio Athletic Conference and as Paul Harvey would say, "*Now the rest of the story*."

On my first night at Wilmington College a very tall, distinguished looking gentleman visited a local Drive-In where the college kids hung out. He walked up to me introducing himself as James Reid--- the new President at Wilmington College. Reid had come to Wilmington from The Kettering Foundation and I was the very first student he met.

Years later, in 1967 when I received my diploma there was an attached hand written note from President Reid that read, *"How ironic is it that the first student I met in 1960 gets the final Diploma I signed before leaving Wilmington College? Congratulations and Good Luck in your chosen field of announcing."*

The Diploma was nice, but that note was priceless and what I will cherish forever.

****

Everyone has that one 'most embarrassing' time in their life that haunts them forever. Mine took place in 1960: the first time I called races for money at The Warren County Fair in Lebanon, Ohio.

It was a short field with only five horses in the race. The two standouts were *Sweet Singer* driven by Charlie Miller and *Terrymite* reined by Eddie Morgan Sr.

The two drivers were opposites: Miller was small in stature and Morgan was quite hefty. (Both donned brown racing colors.) Somehow I got them mixed up and had *Terrymite* winning by open lengths, when it was actually *Sweet Singer*!

The owner of *Terrymite* was Russell Terry who could hear quite well, but his eyesight was poor. Poor Mr. Terry rushed to the winners' circle, beaming from ear-to-ear to get his picture taken--- only to be greeted by Charlie Miller and *Sweet Singer*.

In 1960 I added many county fairs to my resume. During the five years of College I went from calling 5 in 1960 (Lebanon, Urbana, Hamilton, London and Marietta) to a total of 17 by 1965.

That summer I worked 5 racetracks, earning $395 and thought, "*Wow, this is a nice way to make money!*"

****

I started going to The Little Brown Jug in the late 50s. My friend Fremont Whittington would drive us there with lawn chairs in the trunk that we could sit on as we watched the races. We would leave around five in the morning so we would be assured to get a good spot to set up the chairs. If you waited too long you would be out of luck and have to sit way in the back. Of course I never ever imagined I would be calling the races there someday!

After securing our spots along the fence, Fremont and I would buy a race program and walk through the barn area hoping to catch a glimpse of the superstar horses entered in the days' races.

At that time Charlie Hinkle was the race caller and is one of the best announcers in history. Charlie is also another person who has deeply influenced me and helped set my path in Harness Racing.

Years later, in 1967 Charlie called the Adios at The Meadows Racetrack in Washington, Pa. That's when he informed Hank Thomson and Corwin Nixon that he decided to move to California to call professional basketball for singer Pat Boone who owned the team in Los Angeles in the A.B.A.

Corwin thought of me to replace Charlie but couldn't think of my first name: He only knew my last name was Huston and I lived in Xenia. When

Hank got home he called the operator and asked how many Huston's there were in Xenia. She told him there were seven.

Hank started phoning each one in alphabetical order. Ironically, the first call was to a Cecil—my father. Dad gave him my phone number and shortly after 10 p.m. Hank called me.

He said, "*I doubt if you know who I am, but my name is Hank Thomson from Delaware.*"

Needless to say I had never met Hank, but having attended many Jugs in the late 50s and early 60s I knew exactly who he was.

Hank asked if I could call races the first three days and help Stan Bergstein call a few races on Jug Day.

My answer was "*Yes, of course.*"

When I got off the phone my wife Norma asked, "*How much are they paying you?*"

I replied, "*I don't know and I don't care!*"

The racing Gods were smiling down on me, for that was how I got my start of what would become a half-century of calling the famous Standardbred horserace, The Little Brown Jug, in Delaware, Ohio.

Once again I apologize for getting ahead of myself--- for that is another chapter later in the book.

Pompano Park, Pompano Beach, Florida

Pompano Beach, Florida, Pompano Park Night Harness Racing, Exit No. 5 - Sunshine Parkway, "America's Most Beautiful Race Track."

Pompano Park Racetrack Postcard

Pompano Park Announcers Booth

Early 70s

CHAPTER THREE

Pompano Park Racetrack: The Winter Capital Of Harness Racing

Pompano Park Racetrack was the place where horsemen from all over the country flocked during the winter months to train and race their horses. They would leave their hometowns of frigid temperatures and snow to condition their horses in the warm, sunny weather of Florida.

It's much safer to break, train and race a horse in warm weather than in cold, icy conditions. The hard ground can and usually does hurt the horse's hooves, tendons and ligaments. They can slip on the ice, fall and harm themselves; and may even break a bone.

IT STARTED WITH A DREAM

It all started with a dream--- A dream and vision from a man named Frederick Van Lennep--- to build a Standardbred horse track and establish Harness Racing in Florida.

In 1953, Van Lennep, a New York ad executive turned horse breeder noticed from the air a track of land south of Atlantic Boulevard that at one point housed a thoroughbred track. Although he faced formidable legal opposition from various parties with interests in the pari-mutuel business, Van Lennep eventually would develop the "Taj Mahal" of Harness Racing and call it Pompano Park Racetrack.

Van Lennep was also one of the two biggest stockholders in both the historic Red Mile in Lexington, Kentucky and the 79 year-old Tattersalls Sales Company.

He also built Castleton Farms into a leading breeder of quality trotters and pacers.

Van Lennep, a native of Philadelphia married Frances Dodge, heir of the Dodge fortune and owner of Castleton Farm in Kentucky. In 1949 they developed 'Castleton,' turning it into a premier Standardbred nursery.

Van Lennep became increasingly involved in the industry, holding leadership positions in the USTA, Harness Tracks of America, The Hambletonian Society, The Grand Circuit, The American Horse Council and others.

Van Lennep also owned Wolverine Raceway, The Red Mile in Lexington and multiple tracks in Italy.

After discovering the land from an aerial view, he purchased it and converted it to a one-mile harness-training track and officially opened its doors in 1957.

Rightfully deserved, in 1974 Van Lennep was inducted into The Living Hall of Fame.

THE ORIGINAL POMPANO PARK

The grand opening of the original Pompano Park was celebrated on Christmas Day in 1926. Huge crowds of spectators poured into the racetrack on chartered buses from around Florida. The grandstands could easily accommodate 7,000 fans.

In 1928, two years after the track opened, a hurricane ravaged South Florida causing 2,000 fatalities. Pompano Park Racetrack was a savior acting as a Red Cross station to aid more than 1,000 hurricane victims. Subsequently, the track became dormant for 25 years, until 1953 when Van Lennep spotted the track from an airplane.

It wasn't long before many power racing stables shipped into Pompano and trained there, such as: Castleton Racing Stable by Ralph Baldwin, Frank Ervin, Harry Pownall's Arden Homestead and W.W. Vandeveer.

Shortly thereafter, 'The best of the best' would join them, such as: Stanley Dancer, Billy Haughton, Jerry Silverman, Delvin Miller and other Harness Racing elites.

At that time Pompano Park was the place to train and race horses during the winter, although there were a few other training centers such as Spring Garden Ranch and Ben White Raceway that were located in northern Florida.

THE LATE 60s

It was February 4th, 1964—the night thousands of racing fans had been waiting for. It was opening night at the $5.5 million Pompano Park Racetrack. Mother Nature did not cooperate for it had been raining all day making the racetrack condition sloppy. Despite the weather elements, a crowd of 4,011 was in attendance and the handle exceeded $100,000.

That year illustrious Standardbreds named *Speedy Scot, Country Don, Coffee Break, Race Time* and *Kentucky Belle* winter trained at Pompano.

The media and newspapers compared Pompano Park to Las Vegas because people would attend dressed to the nines and dine on fine food in a place that illustrated charm and intimacy.

You could find anyone and everyone at Pompano Park; either dining on an exquisite dinner on the 6th floor or socializing while grabbing a beer and burger at Patton's Place on the 5th floor, hoping to get a tip from a trainer who was hanging out.

On any given morning you could sit in the trackman's kitchen located across from the main track and watch as the trainers exercised their high priced four-legged athletes, often in sets of four or five.

This is what kept horsemen going in this roller coaster sport—the dreams and hopes of owning the next World Champion; and to Miller, Haughton and Dancer, it was no different.

Stanley Dancer, then known as "The Sports Greatest Trainer and Driver" called Pompano Park his home up until 1990. Significant horses in his stable were *Nevele Pride, Most Happy Fella, Albatross, Keystone Ore* and *Super Bowl*-- all who winter trained at Pompano.

The Haughton set featured the likes of *Armbro Omaha, Green Speed, Handle With Care, Nihilator, Romulus Hanover* and *Rum Customer.* These four-legged athletes were among those trained by the man called, "The Master."

I believe it was the year 1962 when Pompano Park re-furbished the training track located behind the track kitchen. Although I hadn't arrived yet I was told every day horsemen enjoyed sitting in the kitchen watching top pilots steer their four-legged athletes—some more easily than others—and wonder who would be the next champion. You had to get there early--- I mean really early--- like by 6 a.m. to even get a seat.

Some feisty colts would bounce up and down like broncos competing in a rodeo, while other mild mannered yearlings jogged along like they had been doing it forever.

Every once in awhile a colt would buck and get his leg over the shaft breaking the piece of wood, but in general all went smoothly.

During the evening Pompano Park would pack in the stands. You never knew whom you might see dining in the clubhouse located on the sixth floor. The likes of Whitey Ford, Jackie Gleason, Rodney Dangerfield, Ed Sullivan, George Steinbrenner, Joe Namath, Pete Rose, Mickey Mantle and Joey Heatherton were some of the celebrities who enjoyed a night at the races.

Notables Minnie Pearl, Mickey Rooney, Walter Matthau, and ole' blue eyes himself, Frank Sinatra, at one time came to Pompano Park to dine and watch the graceful four-legged athletes compete.

Whitey Ford, George Steinbrenner and Arnold Palmer were regulars during the season that eventually became horse and racetrack owners.

Just like people have their favorites in baseball, basketball or football, it was no different in harness racing. Fans would flock to the track to catch a glimpse of the sports' greatest reinsmen—the "Gold Dust Twins"—Stanley Dancer and Billy Haughton.

In 1987 Pompano hosted the $150,000 Invitational Trotting Series that lured five of the six best European trotters to compete in the two-day race series. Horses like 'Aged Trotter of the Year,' *Sugarcane Hanover, Tabor Lobell* and *Express Ride* battled for the trophy.

The 5/8's mile track was composed of Marl: a combination of Florida type clay, concrete sand, and rice rock that is similar to limestone chips or crushed coral. In the middle of the track was a small lake where flamingos and cranes would be soaking and wading.

There had been several situations where horses got spooked and ended up in the lake; but luckily nothing fatal ever happened.

****

During that time my wife Norma and I had just purchased a house in Xenia, so when we made the decision to locate to Florida for the winter our finances were to say the least strapped.

In 1967 I received a call from Dick Wilson, the general manager of Pompano Park Racetrack, asking my schedule for the next few weeks.

He and Bill Van Buren showed up at one of the fairs and heard me announce a race. I looked up and saw Wilson and Van Buren walk in the grandstands when the horses were behind the gate. Trying to do my very best, I got a lump in my throat as 11 of the 12 racehorses broke. I thought to myself, *"Why couldn't they have watched a Free-For-All field of top pacers?"*

I spoke with Van Buren and Wilson all of 30 seconds and looked for them after the races, but they had already left. I was certain I didn't get the job, but all my worrying was in vain when that Saturday I got a telegram offering me the job at Pompano.

I immediately called my parents and Uncle Don. My parents were ecstatic and thought my Uncle would be thrilled, but was stunned when I got a weird response from him.

He said, "*You can't go! You just got married and bought a house.*"

I couldn't understand why Uncle Don didn't want me to go for this was a chance of a lifetime. Confused by my uncles' response I met two of his good friends, Bobby Geyer and Gerald Nash, who I thought a lot of. They both agreed I should take the job for this could be a great opportunity for my career and family.

Four or five years after moving to Florida I discovered why Uncle Don had not been happy for me. One day Dick Wilson, the general manager at Pompano Park, asked me, "*By the way, Rog, do you happen to know a man named Don Huston?*"

Surprised, I answered, "*That's my uncle*" never expecting to hear what Dick was about to say.

"*Well, Don also applied for this job here too.*"

I now understood why Uncle Don didn't want me to take the job!

****

Norma and I bought a small trailer to live in, loaded it with essentials and headed south. We found a nice trailer court not far from the track on N.E.14th Street and set up house.

Once there, Norma got a job at the Harry M. Stevens Catering Service and I got a part-time day job with trainer Marc Ferguson. From 1968 through 1970 I would help Marc jog and train his horses during the day and announce the races at night. I really enjoyed that time and learned a lot about conditioning horses from Marc. He was truly an all around great horseman.

Eventually I took on a third job working with Bob Cox who was the Publicity Director and his wife Ginny who was the secretary. I was young and full of ambition and energy so working three jobs was a piece of cake for me.

During that time Alan J. Finkelson was the Vice President of Public Relations and a major player in the success of the track.

He was a tremendous innovative promoter and would always come up with unique, exciting events to draw in the people.

Alan once set up a match race between a horse and zebra. Trainer/driver Bill Deters sat behind the horse; but I can't recall who drove the zebra.

As it turned out zebras are not as fast as horses, but somehow they managed to make the two animals finish close by each other at the wire. (The horse went a distance of 5/8's and the zebra 1/8 of the mile.)

Alan truly was a genius who came up with 'out of the box' ways to draw in a crowd.

There was the time when Alan set up a match race between a quarter horse and a motorcycle. That was a sight to see; especially when the motorcycle rider revved the engine, scaring the poor horse that wound up crashing into the hub rail, tumbling over with his rider in tow.

At that time Pompano Racetrack also had races for quarter horses which I enjoyed calling. The 'Cowboys' (what we called the trainers) shipped their horses from as far as Texas, Oklahoma, New Mexico and Wyoming.

I liked calling these races, because they were easy, for the horses would race in the straightaway. (At that time I was announcing at Calder in the afternoon and Pompano at night.)

There was a female jockey—one of the very few who stands out in my mind, but unfortunately not in a good way.

When the quarter horse gets behind the gate the jockey will wrap the horses' mane around his hand. As soon as the gate is opened the horse will go the maximum speed—75 mph in the first few strides, before reducing the speed. The horse the female jockey was riding wore a kicking strap.

The kicking strap goes over the horses rear-end and releases when the gate opens. This particular night the strap did not release, thus throwing the female jockey into the air. It was not a pretty sight.

Another story I'd like to share is one concerning a man named Howie Blier. Howie was a die-hard gambler who worked in the Press Box located on the 2nd floor. (The judges' stand and announcers booth was on the floor above the clubhouse.)

One evening Mr. Van Lennep and his wife Frances were dining with friends when their dinner would be interrupted by a freak accident.

There were men we referred to as 'Penguin Alley' who would escort people to their seats after they checked in with the Maitre' D.

Every now and then Howie would get an inside tip from one of the drivers and leave the Press Box to make a bet on the 6th floor clubhouse. That night he was down to his last $5 and didn't want to be shut out so he trekked as fast as he could to the sixth.

In a hurry, Howie dropped the $5 dollar bill and it fell on the ceiling of the walkway. Not realizing that the roof between the floors was 'a false roof,' he put his hands on the railing of the clubhouse and came crashing down landing on top of the assistant Maitre'd.

As dust was flying landing on his dinner plate, Mr. Van Lennep nonchalantly said, *"My God. That's gotta be Hector!"*

Hector was Van Lennep's son, who operated 'Time & Tide'—a place where clocks were made for boats. Of course, it wasn't Hector, but instead Howie.

(Ironically, Hector went on to become the General Manager of Pompano Park.)

****

Yes, I have many wonderful memories that took place during that time in my life at Pompano Park Racetrack: especially the people I met and worked with--- many who are sadly no longer with us.

There are way too many to list, but below I have mentioned several that are dear to my heart.

They include Frederick and Frances Van Lennep, Bill Haughton, Stanley Dancer, George Steinbrenner, Delvin Miller, Glen Garnsey, Archie McNeil, Bill Deters, Tom Wantz, Tom Merriman, Ted Taylor, Sandi Fisher, Dave Rankin, Gary Lewis, Bill Connors, Ken Marshall, Pee Wee Welch, Buck Waugh, Hollis Regur, Sach Werner, Marc Ferguson, Pat Bellows, Lew Williams and Heddy and Bill Nelson.

<u>MY TOP MEMORIES OF RACES AT POMPANO PARK</u>

Moondowner Driver: Bill Pocza First 2:00 mile

Strike Out The Two and Three-Year-Old Florida
Breeders Stake winner.

Doug Ballinger
Greenville, Ohio 1972
My replacement at most County Fairs

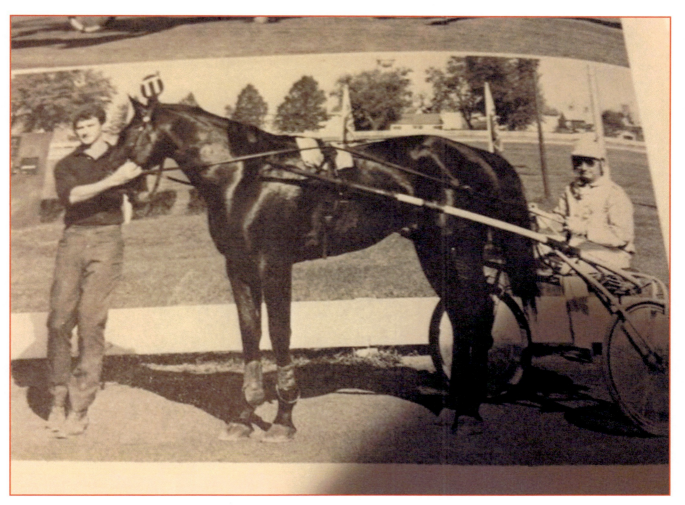

Steady Star's Famous Time Trial

CHAPTER FOUR

The Red Mile

THE RED MILE
60s THROUGH THE 70s

Located in Kentucky, in the heart of the Bluegrass Region is an area that is most famous for horse breeding and racing called Lexington. There you will find one of horseracing's finest racetracks called, The Red Mile Racetrack.

The Red Mile is the second oldest harness track in the world. It simulcasts races 364 days a year and was once the home to The Tattersall Horse Sale. The track is one of the most beautiful tracks in the country and is composed of red clay; thus The Red Miles namesake.

The Red Mile opened its doors on September 28, 1875 with the opening of The Great Fall Trots sponsored by the newly reorganized Kentucky Trotting Horse Breeders Association.

For over 143 years Harness Racings elite has converged on The Red Mile to stage some of the greatest equine battles in history.

I can't go on without writing a little about the history of this spectacular track.

****

The day The Red Mile opened was September 28, 1875. It was just 10 years since President Abraham Lincoln had been shot by stage actor John Wilkes Booth while attending the play *Our American Cousin* at Ford's Theater in Washington, D.C.

When the track first opened The Kentucky Trotting Horse Breeders Association neglected to properly advertise; thus very few people attended the races.

However, after a story was highlighted in the local newspaper, attendance picked up the following day.

In 1893--- The Kentucky Futurity--- The Red Mile's signature event was held. The winner of this auspicious race was a horse named *Oro Wilkes.*

The Red Mile soon gained the reputation for exhilarating, fast-paced races—a reputation that continues to hold today.

It was also the scene of many classic Harness Races and Time Trials, such as *Steady Star* with Joe O'Brien in 1:52.

The initial purpose of Time Trials was to get a fast record on horses for breeding purposes. It should be noted that harness horses known as Standardbreds traditionally were clocked and recorded for their mile performances.

The Red Mile's signature event is The Kentucky Futurity-- a stakes race for three-year-old trotters. It is considered the third jewel in U.S. Harness Racing's Trotting Triple Crown.

The other two are The Hambletonian that is held at The Meadowlands and The Yonkers Trot held at Yonkers Raceway.

Due to The Red Mile's prominent stature in Harness Racing it also hosts prestigious stakes such as: all divisions of The Kentucky Championships, The Bluegrass Stakes, The International Stallion and The Tattersalls Pace.

Besides the racetrack, other facilities at The Red Mile include a modernized two-story clubhouse, a refurbished grandstand, and the round barn that houses memorabilia.

The adjacent Tattersalls Sales Arena no longer hosts horse sales; though the stalls are used for excess ship-in horses.

Well, enough of this. It's just when I get started on the great races and Time Trials, I start babbling.

Now getting back to those memorable years in Lexington.

****

Talk about a hectic schedule. I can't believe how I managed to burn not one candle, but an entire candelabra at both ends, get up the next day and do it all over again. But when you are young you are full of dreams and have an abundant amount of energy.

Even though I try to call as many races as I can today, going from track, to county fairs, to promotions in the 60s and 70s, I was stuck in overdrive.

From 1967 through 1975 I would be in Pompano Park for their winter meet---November to April. Then I would call races at The Red Mile in Lexington, Kentucky from April to June.

During the months of July through September I would go to the county fairs then drive to Delaware, Ohio for The Little Brown Jug during Jug week. After The Jug it was back to Lexington for three weeks and back to sunny Florida.

JEEZ! I'm exhausted just talking about it!

I wasn't the greatest scholar at Wilmington College. My mind was focused more on calling races, than in getting good grades. During that time I acted as both manager and scorekeeper for their basketball games. Shortly after, I took on the job of Sports Information Director and later for The Mid-Ohio Conference, as well as PA Announcer for the football games.

I was also working early mornings at WHBM in Xenia, which had me driving 18 miles to class each day. This is the reason it took me five years to graduate to others' four.

Because of my calling 17 county fairs I was unable to take summer classes. Luckily for me I was given a 'fake' diploma ---only after promising I would do the four hours the next year (which of course got put off a number of years.)

Looking back I realize that throughout my entire life I wasn't fulfilled until my glass was full—No, until it was running over. Today I'm still that way, but maybe just a 'little 'slower. Perhaps that is why I was struck with a heart problem later on in life?

****

When it came to graduating in 1965 I got a D in Biology, which didn't count towards my Minor, thus I was four hours short when Graduation Day came in late April 1965.

As I was driving home from Wilmington College that day, Uncle Don passed me on Rt. 68, motioning me to pull over. He told me as soon as I got home to call Phil Mauger who was the race announcer at The Red Mile Racetrack in Lexington, Kentucky.

My mind started to wander, questioning why I should call Mr. Mauger. Of course I knew of The Red Mile, as anyone who has anything to do with horseracing does.

The minute I walked in the house I called Phil who asked if I would fill in the final week of the Spring Meet. Of course I said yes!

However, there was a little problem. When I asked the owner of the radio station for a week off, to my surprise he said "no" for he didn't have a replacement.

At first I was mad, but that wouldn't solve anything so after a few minutes I came up with a solution. I would work my shift of 5 a.m. to1 p.m., run home to take a nap, and then drive 147 miles to The Red Mile.

I'd announce a 10 race card, drive back home, get a few winks and start the day over again. I don't know how I did that but I did, for five straight days!

I forgot to mention that the first night I arrived at The Red Mile I went to The Clubhouse to introduce myself to the general manager, Walter Gibbons. It wasn't hard finding him for he always wore a large, white cowboy hat.

Mr. Gibbons told me to take a seat and asked if I wanted a drink. I sat down and replied, *"Just a glass of water,"* which he remarked, *"Young man, you will go a long way in this business."*

****

The week I called the races, once again Mother Nature did not cooperate or make my job easy for it rained every single day. At that time the drivers didn't have rain colors: they all wore green or brown raincoats which made it more difficult to differentiate one driver from the other.

The track conditions were very bad, thus the fastest race the entire week was 2:40!

In 1966 Phil asked me to work the final three weeks, but I had little time to prepare. I got a weeks vacation from the radio station so I would drive back and forth the first and third week and got a room the second week at The Old Springs Motel.

For a young man who had only announced county fairs in Ohio it was a big step to call races with some of the biggest stars in the sport such as: Howard Beissinger, Sonny Graham, Billy Herman, Frank Ervin, Ralph Baldwin, Charlie Clark, Donnie Miller, Ned Bower and many more.

I could name at least 50 more that drove every night, such as: Don McKirgan, Dave Howard, Fred Bach, Dennis Lacey, Alvin Tucker, Gary Mills, Mike Arnold, Bob Burnett, Brooks Wells, Odell Thompson, Charlie Jordan, Jan Johnson, Carl Allen, Bill Popfinger, Joe Adamsky and Gerald Russell.

In 1967 everything fell into place for this young, ambitious announcer when I was hired to call races at Pompano Park, The Red Mile (full time in Spring and Fall) and of course The Little Brown Jug in Delaware.

This all took place within a three-week period. (By the way, I did this, along with calling a few fairs in Ohio from 1967 through 1975).

****

During that time at Lexington I had the opportunity to work alongside some of the best in the business. In Publicity there was Bob and Ginny Cox, Tom White and Russell Rice.

The General Manager was Biff Lowry and the Judges were Walter Russell, Ed Casey and Chester Boyle. The soundman was Claude Cashman, the race secretary was Gary Buxton, the Paddock Judge was Al Brown, the Photo Finish was Gerald and Bob Nash, and the starters were Paul Young and Tom Eaton.

That is when the GM Biff Lowry along with Tom White and myself came up with a 'Pick 8' in the 8th race. The idea was to pick the exact order of finish of the 8th race on a given night for 10 straight weeks.

The first week a $100 prize would be awarded. If nobody won the second week $200 would be awarded and if there was still no winner it would build up until there was a winner. By 10 weeks it would rise to a $1,000 prize.

When it was over we had a total of 21 winners, as I had picked the morning line in the exact order of finish. But there was one problem. In making the rules Biff forgot to say, "*In the event of multiple winners, they would share equally.*"

In forgetting to clarify this The Lexington Trots Breeders Association grudgingly had to pay out $21,000 that night.

The controller (whose name escapes me) was livid---but we had a number of ecstatic fans.

Every time I would see Tom White we would relive that evening.

****

As far as races that stood out in my mind during that time was *Bertha Parker* who had the first sub 2:00 mile under the lights and *Bret Hanover* with Frank Ervin winning their two-year-old debut.

Also were *Colonial Charm* and Glen Garnsey, *Dream of Glory* and Pius Soehnlen, *Kentucky* and Bruce Nickells, *Arnie Almahurst* with driver Joe O'Brien for trainer Gene Riegle, and *Handle With Care* and William Haughton.

However, one of my biggest memories was the many Time Trials that took place at Lexington.

In the late 60s Biff Lowry approached me to be The Time Trial Director at The Red Mile. The idea was to promote Time Trials at $50 a Trial. (If they went during the racing program, it was $200).

I don't have the exact figures but when we started in 1969 I think we had over 100 Time Trials with Fred Bach driving the prompter. It steadily grew to over 1,200 by 1975 with others getting into the prompting business, including Shine Ogan and Dennis Lacey.

When we ran ads in the horse magazines it really took off. My office of what I remember was the old and unused security office that led into the barn area.

Thus, many premium stallions or mares were measured against the clock. Some that still carry Time Trial marks are *Rodney, Fancy Crown, Most Happy Fella, Yankee Lass, Bye-Bye Byrd, Dancer Hanover, Dayan, Hickory Pride, Isle of Wight, Steady Beau* and *Sampson Direct*.

Certain drivers specialized in handling the time for Time Trialing horses, while others were good with the prompters. When *Adios Butler* knocked 2/5's off *Billy Direct's* twenty-two-year-old 1:55 clocking, owner Paige West drove the four-year-old, while Delvin Miller and driver/trainer Eddie Cobb drove the thoroughbred prompters.

Frank Ervin put a 1:57 mark on the then five-year-old *Adios* in a Time Trail when he was offered $500 to break the track record, and four years later the great *Gene Abbe* Time Trialed in 2:00.3.

****

Time Trials became very important and trainers would schedule their Time Trial. Depending on the numbers we had we would start as early as 9 a.m. in the morning and go through noon each day. (We could usually handle from 10 to 12 Time Trials per hour.)

During the races we would have one after each race; saving the fastest miles for the afternoon session of racing.

The most sought after driver was (Jigglin) Joe O'Brien—sometimes having as many as thirty drives in a morning session.

In 1972 everyone was talking about four-year-old *Steady Star* who was going to break *Bret Hanover's*, 1:53.2 World Record.

Each morning Joe would arrive at my office at 6:30 a.m. right on the minute to check what Time Trials he had that day and as to who and when they were scheduled.

At that time there were several horses and trainers O'Brien never heard of, but to my knowledge Gentleman Joe never turned one down.

Each morning I would ask him the same question, *"Are you going with Steady Star today?"* His answer was always the same, *"No, not today. The conditions have to be 'perfect.'"*

We were down to the last few days left in the meet and on that particular morning the fog was so dense it took me a good 20 minutes to get to the office. When I arrived, Joe was anxiously waiting for me. I never thought this would be 'the day' I had been waiting for.

After checking his schedule O'Brien asked me, *"Aren't you going to ask me about Steady Star?"* I was taken back for I was pretty sure the Time Trials would be cancelled and post time for the races would be delayed until the fog lifted, but as they say, "The show must go on," and it did.

Joe assured me that this was the day for *Steady Star* to break the record and the track conditions would be perfect by the 5 p.m. Post Time.

There was only one condition: He didn't want me to announce he was going to go the mile with *Steady Star* and would let me know for certain by 5 p.m.

4 o'clock went by and there was no word from Joe. Finally, around 4:30 O'Brien called and said, *"We will go after the last race, but don't announce it until you actually see me on the track."*

The last race on the card had finished and the enthusiastic crowd of over 2,500 made their way to the parking lot. With maybe only 100 fans left in the stands, O'Brien appeared on the track with *Steady Star.*

I cleared my throat and announced, *"Now on the track trying to break the world record of Bret Hanover is Joe O'Brien and Steady Star!"*

The people in the parking lot behind the grandstand ran back to view the famous Time Trial and the rest is history!

That day O'Brien and *Steady Star* broke the World Record in Harness Racing in a mile of 1:52-----witnessed by not more than 750 lucky fans and a number of trainers, drivers and caretakers.

Several years later, the owner of *Steady Star*, Chester Ault, called me and wanted to do something special for his champion horse. We came up with the idea of getting material that could be made into curtains, bedspreads, and even sport jackets.

On the material would be a picture of four horses: *Steady Star, Handle With Care, Albatross* and *Delmonica Hanover*; and a picture of a stopwatch displaying *Steady Star's* winning mile of 1:52.

Also, there would be a picture of The Hambletonian Trophy, The Little Brown Jug, The Adios Trophy and The Stable of Memories.

I still have the curtains and sports jacket today, although I can no longer fit into it.

Those were some of the best memories I have of The Red Mile. It was a great time for I met super people and watched and called champion horses.

Racing at The Red Mile is still going strong, where records are being broken every year. In the year 2000, Tattersalls and The Red Mile was sold to five Standardbred breeders dedicated to the revitalization of the racetrack and sales pavilion. A major renovation nicknamed, "The Red Mile Renaissance" began and will be ongoing for the next few years.

Sam McKee inducted to The Communicators Hall of Fame
2012

Sam McKee, *left, chats with his "teacher"* **Roger Huston.**

Sam McKee (age 14) at Delaware
1976

CHAPTER FIVE

Sam McKee: My Friend and Protege

SAM MCKEE

3/24/62   3/10/17

"NEVER STAND IN THE WAY OF A YOUNG PERSON IN WHAT THEY WANT TO DO BECAUSE YOU NEVER KNOW WHO THEY MIGHT TURN OUT TO BE."

Roger Huston

As I talk about this very special man my eyes instantly tear up. The person I am talking about is *Sam McKee*, my good friend who we sadly lost in 2017. It was a great loss to not only Harness Racing but to the world.

I feel compelled to write a chapter in honor of Sam for he was and always will be a very important part of my life.

I am the proud father of two daughters, Cami Sue and Nevele, and stepson Troy, but if there was ever a young man who I considered my own, it was Sam.

He was a man who never one day was down or depressed. He was always upbeat, happy and kind to everyone he met.

Sam grew up on a farm where he trained and raced horses with his father and grandfather. His immense passion for Harness Racing goes unmatched to the love of his family.

Ours was a love story that started when he was six-years-old.

Sam knew at that young age exactly what he wanted to do with his life: To be an announcer of horseraces and that's exactly what he did. Not only in my opinion, but also many others—he was one of the best!

When he was ten-years-old Sam began writing me letters, which I answered each and every one. After several years he began sending cassette tapes where he called the races at the Michigan fairs from the back of the grandstand.

In the early 70s I met Sam at The Little Brown Jug after he sent me a note. We instantly bonded. I believe he was fourteen-years- old at the time, but I knew the minute I met him I was looking at a young man who one day would be a Super Star in Harness Racing. The passion, ambition and enthusiasm he had was nothing I had ever seen in anyone before.

I believe it was May or June of 1976 when Sam wrote me saying he would like to come visit me at The Meadows. I told him he could stay at my house with my wife Norma and daughter Cami Sue.

Sam hitched a ride to our house from Michigan and arrived the next week, immediately fitting in as one of our family.

On that visit he called his very first race. It was the National Youth Driving Race, won by Ron Newhart.

I wanted to help this young man but didn't know how to so I called Bobby Williams the race superintendent at the Clinton County Fair and asked him to give Sam a try. When Bobby heard he was only 14 he said, *"I don't want to pay a kid $50 to call races."* But he did.

Sam didn't need mine, or anyone's help, for he quickly made a name on his own. He began announcing the County Fairs and eventually graduated to race meets at Toledo, Sports Creek, and Saginaw. Shortly later he got a job as announcer at Ladbroke in Detroit, and finally The Red Mile and The Meadowlands Racetrack.

Sam and I were much more than friends—we were like father and son.

I remember going up to Flint, Michigan, one time with my wife and daughter and stayed with Sam's family.

He took me on my first snowmobile ride--- something I will never forget.

Besides the love of announcing races we had a lot of things in common. I discovered that as a young boy Sam did the same thing I did. We both built racetracks with toy horses and would call races. We would roll the dice to see how many strides the horse would go.

It came as a shock to his family, friends and harness racing family when out of the blue Sam had a stroke at the young age of 54.

While Sam's work credentials are impressive, they still pale in comparison to the man and friend he was. There was never anyone more thoughtful, generous, kind and whose enthusiasm was more infectious.

Sadly, I never got to say "good-bye," but in a way I'm glad I didn't. Although those close to him thought he would survive the massive stroke, I didn't. I prayed and prayed he would recover, but the severity of it overtook him.

His death is one of the hardest things I have ever gone through. In fact, please don't take this the wrong way but I had a harder time dealing with his death than with my own parents. Probably because he was so young and it was sudden.

I want to remember the good times we had. I know someday we will be together again for Sam was also a believer. In fact, I'm sure he's calling races up in Heaven right now, entertaining everyone and now sees his Savior face-to-face.

I look forward to that fine day when I will see Sam again and the sorrow of his parting will be gone forever.

For the longest time—almost a year--- every time I would call a race, Sam would come into my thoughts and I had to do everything I could not to break down.

We all grieve in our own way and for me I want to think of the good times. I was asked and honored to give the eulogy at Sam's funeral.

I found a poem that was written by an unknown author, but it describes exactly how I feel. This one's for you, my friend!

I AM FREE

Be not burdened with times of sorrow
I wish you the sunshine of tomorrow.
My life's been full-- I've savored much
Good friends, good times, a loved one's touch.

Perhaps my time seemed all too brief
Don't lengthen it now with undue grief.
Lift up your heart and share with me
God called me now
He set me free!

-----In Memory of Sam McKee-----

The resting place of the great ADIOS
Meadow Lands Farm, Pennsylvania

The Announcers Booth at The Meadows

*Lori Romanettie, Marcie and Pastor Joe DiDonato, me, and Lee
Alphen of The Christian Harness Horsemen's Association*

The Meadows Winning Trifecta
Jerry Erenstein, Trish Schaut & me

My TV and Co-Hosts
Jack O'Connor, Jeff Zidek, Jim Sciulli and Evan Pattak

*Herve Filion and Dave Palone--The day Palone broke
Herve's Win Record.*

Dave Palone and I sharing an emotional moment after he broke The World's Record for Most Wins.

CHAPTER SIX

The Meadows

It was the beginning of 1976. That is the year I suppose you could say I relocated to a place that would become my Forever Home---The Meadows Racetrack--- the oldest harness track overall in Pennsylvania.

I was sitting at my desk in the Publicity Office at Pompano Park in December 1974 when Delvin Miller, owner of The Meadows Racetrack in Meadow Lands, Pa. called and asked if I was interested in moving to Pennsylvania.

At first I thought, *"Pennsylvania year round! That meant snow, frigid temperatures and icy roads. I had enough of that growing up in Ohio. Anyways, how could anyone leave sunny Florida for frigid, snowy Pennslvania?"*

As I looked out the window I saw sunny skies, horsemen walking around in shorts and t-shirts, and this was December. There was no snow on the track, the horsemen didn't don winter attire, and the horses didn't have icicles hanging from their whiskers.

But this was a 'once-in-a-lifetime' golden opportunity! To be able to call races year-round meant my family no longer had to pick up every couple months and re-locate like travelling gypsies. The packing and moving and doing it all over again, was stressful on everyone!

For the past nine years I shuffled my family from Lexington, Kentucky, working at The Red Mile to Pompano Racetrack in Florida. My daughter Cami Sue was now 7-years- old and it was time for her to have a stable home. I didn't like what unfortunately many horsemen had to do--- take their children out of a school and friends they know to move to another.

Also, I wasn't thrilled with having to give up calling races at my beloved Ohio fairs for quarter horseracing at Pompano every summer.

After talking it over with my wife, Norma, I called John Townsend who just happened to be Delvin Miller's nephew. After talking with Mr. Townsend I agreed to visit The Meadows once they resumed their 1975 racing season.

During our conversation I discovered that Joe Hardy, the owner of 84 Lumber, had heard me announce races at Pompano Park and liked what he heard so suggested they offer me the job at The Meadows. Mr. Hardy's partner and close friend was Ed Ryan of Ryan Homes.

In April 1975, I made the trip to Western Pennsylvania to The Meadows. I knew that the prestigious race for top three-year-old pacing colts called, The Adios, was held there every year.

On my visit to The Meadows I instantly fell in love with the place and the people who were the kindest and most congenial group. I talked to Mr. Townsend and told him I would love to take the job and could start the 1976 season. He told me he would get back to me in a couple weeks.

Several weeks went by and I didn't hear anything from Mr. Townsend or anyone else concerning the job until the final Saturday of the Lexington fall meet. Of course I was disappointed and wondered why I hadn't been contacted.

That day Mr. Ryan showed up with one of his colts he brought there to Time Trial. Out of curiosity I asked him whatever happened to the offer to be the announcer at The Meadows, since I hadn't heard a thing since the April meeting.

Mr. Ryan was shocked and told me he thought everything was settled and I would be working at The Meadows in February 1976. He assured me as soon as he got home he would call Joe Hardy about the situation.

The next Tuesday there was a knock on my door at my Coconut Creek home around 5 p.m. It was Joe Hardy who flew down to Florida to talk with me personally.

My wife Norma and I invited Joe to stay for dinner. He accepted and we talked which lasted into the late evening. Joe explained they were in the process of putting a whole new team to work at The Meadows, which needed a big push for year round racing.

We talked until 1 a.m. I knew it was either time to have Joe arrested for trespassing or agree to take the job. Of course, I told him I would take the job.

Now came the hard part. I had to tell my friends and fellow workers at Pompano Park that I was leaving. I decided to tell them the news on Halloween. Don't ask me why I chose that day.

I arranged a meeting with Hector Van Lennep, the son of Fred Van Lennep, who was now the General Manager.

He was shocked to say the least and not very happy with my decision, so I told him I would stay on until the early January 1975-76 racing season.

On my last day working at Pompano I got an invitation to have dinner in the Clubhouse with Allen Finkelson and a guest. When I arrived at the clubhouse Allen and his guest greeted me; who just happened to be George Steinbrenner. I knew who Steinbrenner was; he was the owner and managing partner of the New York Yankees. Needless to say, I didn't get a word in the entire night. (And that says something--- for me not to be able to talk!) During our meeting Alan informed me my replacement would be a man named Jerry Glantz.

It was Sunday, January 4th, in the middle of a blinding snowstorm when I arrived in Pittsburgh. When I stepped off the plane and saw the weather I thought to myself, *"I sure hope I did the right thing!"*

That Monday I met the entire team at The Meadows. There was Tom Rooney the Publicity Director; Hunt Garner who was known as Mr. Meadows; Tom Charters the Assistant Race Secretary and Bob Freed of The Harry M. Stevens Company. During that meeting Rooney informed me I would be contacted by a Pittsburgh radio personality to be a guest on his talk show that evening. The man's name was Myron Cope.

Tom informed me that Mr. Cope's voice was squeaky and you never knew what could come out of his mouth! He also warned me Mr. Cope was 'a little off the wall.' (Myron also worked with Jack Fleming and Bill Hillgrove on the Steelers Radio Network)

The interview with Myron turned out to be very enjoyable, yet different, to say the least. He was a great guy who became a friend of mine.

****

There are two stories I want to share about Myron Cope.

Myron told me he always wanted to announce a horse race so I told him, "No problem." I said I would whisper into his ear what to say and he could repeat if he needed help.

Well it turned out that he indeed needed help, but forgot to mention he couldn't hear in his right ear.

The other story is the time when he was a driver in a celebrity match race and there was an equipment glitch. The tie down broke, shifting one shaft of the sulky up in the air.

But determined to win, Myron urged his horse on. He finished second but we decided then that all match races would be performed in a two-seated Jog Cart and the participants riding with a professional driver.

****

Opening night took place on Friday, February 6, 1976. The night before, I met Delvin's wife, Mary Lib Miller. When I first saw her she was down on her hands and knees trying to get a spot off the Clubhouse carpet. From that night on Mary Lib and I were great friends. In fact, I was honored to give the eulogy at her funeral years later.

Before she died I had a heartfelt interview concerning her life, at her request. The entire interview is at The Hall of Fame, in Goshen.

Mary Lib was a great lady and she and Delvin made a terrific team. They both were instrumental to Harness Racing in a big way.

****

If I were a superstitious person and it was any indication what my career would be like at The Meadows, I may have quit before I ever got started for the weather did not cooperate (to say the least) opening night. That night one of the most severe ice storms ever to hit Western Pennsylvania decided to visit--- thus the races were cancelled

However, Joe Hardy and Ed Ryan had invited around 200 guests who actually showed up in the inclement weather, so they asked me to call 'fake' races for the crowd.

I did and they loved it! The next night the weather cooperated and we officially opened the doors for the season.

****

In the early 80s William King developed live coverage of racing at Lousiville Downs and his own system of wagering for home viewers.

At that time the Meadows was owned by Delvin Miller, Ed Ryan and Joe Hardy. They were looking for ways to take Harness Racing to a new audience and introduced them to wagering from their own living room.

One summer evening at Froggy's Restaurant and Bar in Downtown Pittsburgh, a meeting was held between Hardy, Ryan, General Manager Terry Bove and Nelson Goldberg of TCS Sports. The idea was to develop a show and have it air on cable television that served homes in the Pittsburgh area. We were starting from scratch.

At that time Nelson Goldberg of TCS Sports was the gentleman behind the broadcast of Penn State Football. During that meeting Nelson outlined what would be needed on the trackside and what he could offer on the broadcast side.

The hope was to get the broadcast on Warner Amex which we all thought would be the most difficult for it would air five nights a week from 7 to 11 p.m., which was prime time.

(This was before the idea of a cable company having 200 or more channels to choose from.)

During the meeting I suggested a format that is basically as it is with todays broadcast.

The next thing was to find a host from the Pittsburgh TV market of which would be narrowed down to three choices.

The consensus was it would be very difficult for they all had day jobs and wouldn't want to be tied up with a five night a week gig year round.

About that time Joe Hardy was chomping on a cigar (his signature trademark) and asked, *"Why can't Roger do it?"*

I wasn't expecting that curve ball to be thrown at me!

My response: *"A couple things would also have to be added to The Meadows operation: Primarily an assistant announcer to make regular announcements and act as a go-between with the judges. And there would have to be TV crew.* (4 cameras, audio, graphics, videotape, a director and assistant in the booth)

The main thing to be added at the track was a studio on top of the grandstand. (By the way, this was somehow overlooked until about three weeks before airtime.)

Thus, the first studio was a building 15 feet-deep which had windows, a sliding door to separate the regular announcing, and a backdrop for the pre-show which was a map of The United States. The reason for that was so we could put a stickpin on the map representing viewers from all over the States and Canada. We would put up our signal nightly for the whole world to see, as the signal in the early days was not encrypted.

Our first broadcast was on Tuesday, November 1, 1983 and my co-host was Jerry Connors. The well-traveled Jerry had worked for the U.S.T.A. and several racetracks as Publicity Director.

The remainder of the weeks show was filled with Mary Calabrese the Call-A-Bet Director, and Charlie Bishop our Race Secretary.

Since we didn't have a regular co-host for the show it was decided to have various persons who were involved in the sport, including my co-author Vicki Porco (Howard) who was the first woman co-host. (At the time, Vicki was a trainer/owner)

Over the years, Vicki and I also did numerous commercials for Howard Motors. To say the least, they were entertaining and pleasing to the eye.

Over the years we interviewed many owners, trainers, caretakers and fans alike. Two in particular stand out for me. The first being owner Bob Key, who in my opinion should be inducted to The Harness Hall of Fame.

I remember one of the questions I asked Bob was, "*How much money he spends yearly in stake payments?*" His answer was, "*In excess of a million dollars.*" And this was in the 80s!

Another interview that stands out was Paul Norris, the father of trainer-driver Charlie Norris, who told the story of being struck by lightning during a post parade at Lebanon Raceway.

One of the fans that joined the show on a regular basis was Jerry Finn. Jerry first introduced me to Pittsburgh Sports personality, Stan Savran, who came to this market at the same time in 1976, as we both made the move from Ohio.

For a living Jerry sold Kitchenware utensils to hotels, restaurants, and also to The Meadows.

Jerry was also a regular on Myron Copes' talk show on WTAE where he was known as Zivko Kovalchek. He was very knowledgeable in Harness Racing but was also a very funny guy who when on the air was a true Zivko, thus developed quite a following on The Meadows Racing Network.

We did a number of In-House commercials, promoting Call-A-Bet wagering and other track promotions.

Some memorable ones include driver/trainer Dean Zaimes driving his corvette to the entrance at The Meadows. He slammed on the brakes to a screeching halt; Zivko got out of the car and ran into the Call-A-Bet window to open an account with the secret password, "Kobassi."

Another was a spoof on John Cameron Swayze and watches. The Meadows was giving away a watch and the spot was to tape it to a sulky wheel attached to a horse driven by Dean Zaimes.

Zaimes made a few turns on the track and then came back to the winners' circle to have Zivko pointing out that the watch was still ticking. Zaimes then took off for the paddock with Zivko chasing him, yelling he wanted his watch back.

The only problem was Corwyn Green, our trackman at the time, had scraped the track and the goo was lying on the outside.

Zivko never missed a step running in the goo but in the process his shoe was pulled off his foot!

****

There came a time when we wanted a regular co-host on a nightly basis. One of our track regulars named Jerry Erenstein, started doing some barn interviews that would air on that night's broadcast and did an exceptional job.

Thus, Erenstein was hired as our first full time co-host. Jerry was a man of many catch phrases, such as, "*Treading in quicksand*," and "*He folded up like a cheap suitcase.*" (Referring to a horse in the race that stopped quickly)

Jerry remained with us until his passing in the late 90s. He was one of the most well liked men in the business and his loss was felt and still is by many.

Others who appeared regularly were Kevin Decker, Bob Sabot, Jim Jefferson, Bernie Caplan, Frank Kukurin, Nick Salvi, Dr. Bob Pfingsler, Carrie Flickinger and Tony McGrew.

The brightest and most informative addition was Trish Schaut who worked for us from 1992-1996. Trish came to us from Maywood. We were lucky to get her, especially since Phil Langley of Sportsman Park advised her not to take the job.

Trish, being a horsewoman with great knowledge of the sport, added so much with her paddock interviews on a nightly basis.

We also combined to do a weekly Ladbroke Racing Wire-to-Wire, which covered all of racing in the states.

At present we have four very knowledgeable individuals doing the show with me on a weekly basis. The first is Jim Scuilli, who won a contest on KDKA radio when Steve Talbot was conducting a contest to fulfill a persons dream.

Scuilli's dream was to call a race at The Meadows. His wish was fulfilled in June of 1983, even prior to our Meadows Racing Network. In his debut Jim called a race at The Meadows that was won by the horse *Italian Lover* driven by J.C. Miller. He did such a great job that he joined the broadcast in 1985.

Another great co-host is Jeff Zidek who has served The Meadows in various categories since joining in 1988. He joined the TV Broadcast and has become my back-up announcer; a position he still holds today.

Jack O'Connor became part of the show in 1999 when the track decided to have a simulcast show in the daytime and at nights when we weren't racing.

Evan Pattak started with The Meadows when he began doing releases for the track on its many racing activities. Evan is a co-host along with being the paddock interviewer and was lucky to have handled the retirement of the great racehorse *Foiled Again.*

Over the years we have called The Meadows races from a wide variety of locations: To be exact, 35 in all. They include 22 in Pennsylvania, 4 in Virginia, 3 in Ohio, 2 in New Jersey and 1 each in Florida, Michigan, Maryland and Indiana. Of course they began after The Meadows Racing Network got underway.

The initial one was in 1985 when I couldn't get a backup to call the races. With our satellite signal there were many home viewers.

The occasion was my parents 50th Wedding Anniversary, so the solution was to do our first live remote broadcast from their home in Xenia, Ohio.

The audience consisted of 50 family and friends, along with 2 TV stations and 3 newspaper writers.

To our knowledge this had never been attempted, but were pleasantly surprised it went off without a hitch, except for the last race when a severe lightning storm hit The Meadows and we lost the signal.

John Hudock, who was the assistant GM at The Meadows, stepped up and called the final race at the track.

Dr. Scott Woogen, a gentleman who is very instrumental in Harness Racing in Virginia used our remotes to promote Harness Racing at the 3 off-track locations in the state, before racing at Colonial Downs. These remotes were also very good promotional tools for the sport, as it gave us the opportunity to get out and meet the fans.

Last, but certainly not least, is Sandie Penvose Green. When I first came to The Meadows Sandy was secretary to Tom Rooney, our Publicity Director. Over the years she became my back-up announcer. It all started with a Powder Puff Race (all female drivers) when she wanted to announce; and announce she did, without any help from me.

At one time Freehold was looking for an announcer and Stan Bergstein recommended Sandie. She ultimately turned the job down because she was married with children.

I'm very proud of our Meadows family: The trainers, drivers, owners and employees, along with one-time Director of Racing, Kevin Decker. They are a devoted, loving bunch of great people.

The Meadows was also the launching place for several harness race superstars who either call The Meadows home, got their start there, or it was a steppingstone in their careers. They are Dave Palone, Brian Sears, Richard Stillings, The Burke's, Dave Miller, Rodney Bolon, Ben Bolon, and Aaron Merriman.

Throughout the years I have witnessed young men like Dave Palone, Brian Zendt, Rodney Bolon, Tyler Stillings, Mike Wilder, Dan Rawlings, Lew Keith and J.C. Miller Jr. become very good drivers.

I've watched as Mickey Burkes' two sons, Ron and Mickey Jr. evolve into one of harness racing's all-time top conditioners with countless World Champions.

People who were and are my good friends who call The Meadows home are Ed Ryan (once the owner of the track and Ryan Homes) Joe Hardy, owner of horses and also 84 Lumber Company and Nemacolin Woodlands; Roy Davis, the owner of the great Spur horses and of course Delvin Miller, the founder of The Meadows Racetrack and trainer of many, many great horses, including *Adios.*

Adios was Delvin's favorite horse. Since The Meadows' biggest race is named after *Adios* and he is a 'legend' and our track mascot, I feel the need to talk a little about this great stallion.

(See Chapter 8 for more about The Adios Race and winners)

****

Adios was born on January 3, 1940 at Two Gaits Farm in Indiana. At the time he was trained by Frank Ervin and for a short while owned by Harry Warner of Warner Brothers.

The colt was on the small size in stature, but had a heart bigger than his body. In 1948 Delvin purchased *Adios* to stand stud at his Meadow Lands Farm. He proved to be a fantastic stallion and considered by many to be the greatest in Harness Racing.

Adios sired 8 Little Brown Jug winners and his sons *Adios Butler* and *Bret Hanover* both became winners of The Triple Crown of Harness Racing for Pacers.

Before he died in 1965 *Adios* had sired 589 offspring. He was laid to rest under his favorite apple tree near the paddock that had been his home for 17 years.

A race is named after him that is held at The Meadows on the last Saturday in July every year. It has evolved into one of the most important events in Harness Racing.

'The Delvin Miller Adios Pace for the Orchids' is the most prestigious stakes race at the track and when pulling into the entrance there is a life-size statue of *Adios* to greet you.

Back in those days Miller would throw the best party during Adios week. It would be held in a barn where 200-300 people would attend. Both horsemen and celebrities made an appearance such as Stan Musial, Arnold Palmer, Whitey Ford, Boots Randolph, Eddie Arcaro and Tonto aka/Jay Silverheels.

(The draw for the Adios would also be held in The Adios Room.) One time I met and sat with one of my childhood idols, Buffalo Bob Smith of Howdy Doody fame. I was in awe to be talking to someone I grew up watching.

****

Times have changed and although it may be hard it is said that change is good. Perhaps it is, but I really miss the way The Meadows once was.

It is still a great track and I'm proud to be here, but today it is much different than when I first came. There is a huge casino that displays 65 table games, 3,000 slot machines and 14 poker tables.

Situated in various locations throughout the Racino are great restaurants such as Bistecca, The Carvery, The Band Wagon, Far East Noodles, Delvins, The Pub, CB, and a food court.

We have our own bowling alley and provide 5 star headliner shows and special events throughout the year.

We even have our own chapel that is open to the public where our Sunday and holiday services are run by Pastor Joe Di Donato.

I am now ready to begin my 44th year at The Meadows. During that time I have worked with some of the greatest people in the business.

Nine different groups have owned The Meadows since 1976. I have watched as we have gone from a racetrack to The Meadows Race Track and Casino.

Yes, a lot of things have changed, but I can say it has been one hell of a great ride!

I will end this chapter of my life by saying that my friend Sandie Penvose Green in her final days of life called me and said, "*Get your ass over here to my house. I want to say goodbye.*" During the time of her cancer I couldn't get up enough courage to go and see her.

I visited her that day for well over two hours and she passed a few days later. Sandie is another dear friend who I miss but will see again one day.

CURRENT STAKE RACES AT THE MEADOWS

The Delvin Miller Adios Pace for the Orchids

This is the signature event for three-year-old pacers. It has been raced every year since 1967. It is held in July.

The Adioo Volo

The Adioo Volo is part of the Grand Circuit week. This race is the equivalent to the Adios, but is for three-year-old fillies. It is held in July during Adios week.

Arden Downs

Part of Grand Circuit week, the Arden Downs is for two-year-old-filly pacers, filly trotters and three-year-old fillies, colts and gelding trotters.

Currier & Ives

The Currier & Ives is a race for three-year-old open trotters held in May and June.

Pennsylvania Fair Finals

Held in October, the Pa. Fair Finals is a combination for two and three-year-old geldings, colts and filly trotter and pacers.

Keystone Classic

Also held in October is The Keystone Classic. It is a combination of two and three-year-old colt, gelding and filly trotters and pacers.

Brown Jug Race, Delaware County Fair
Delaware, Ohio

Aerial view of The Little Brown Jug
Delaware, Ohio
Late 50s

*Susie Dupler-Telle, owner of Big Bad John accepting Jug Trophy
from Tom Thomson
2011 'Little Brown Jug Winner'*

Butch Green
Caretaker of The Little Brown Jug – The Log Cabin
Delaware 2018

Sitting in the Announcer's Booth at Delaware
2017

Diane Winters and Ethin & Susie Dupler-Telle
The Parade at Delaware Ohio

Susie Dupler-Telle helping me at T-Shirt signing
Delaware, Ohio

Hank Thomson
Co-Founder of The Little Brown Jug

Races at The Fryeburg Fair

CHAPTER SEVEN

The Little Brown Jug

THE LITTLE BROWN JUGS

In the sport of Harness Racing The Little Brown Jug is known as The Super Bowl of Harness Racing. Raced every September at Delaware, Ohio the race is the premier pacing classic for three-year-olds.

For more than a half-century the race has drawn thousands of racing fans yearly. It began in 1937 when the Delaware Ohio County Fairgrounds voted to move the County Fair to Delaware on a tract of land situated at the northern edge of the city.

The Little Brown Jug was formed to stage the Grand Circuit meeting, but the actual birth of this famous race was named through a newspaper contest with previews in 1944 and 1945.

On opening Jug Day in 1946, the purse was $35,358 and won by ***Ensign Hanover*** with "Curly" Smart in the sulky.

When the day finally arrived, parking lots were full by mid-morning. 27,000 fans, trainers, drivers and owners came from Ohio to Canada. That day there were four grueling heats (Yes, four!) before declaring *Ensign Hanover* the victor where he returned to the winners' circle where he was draped with a wreath of roses. In the final heat there were three horses: two colts and one filly.

From the very beginning the steeply banked Delaware track, built by Rollie McNamara was lightning fast and highly accepted by the horsemen.

In this chapter I will talk about a few Jugs that were special to me or I think needs touched on.

In 1947 ***Forbes Chief*** won The Jug with driver Del Cameron in 2:05, and the next year in 1948 ***Knight Dream*** with Frank Safford took home the trophy in 2:07.1, making his sire *Nibble Hanover* the only horse to sire both a Jug and Hambletonian winner. In 1949 it would be ***Good Time*** with Frank Ervin.

In 1950 **Dudley Hanover** driven by Delvin Miller won in 2:03.2, and in 1951 the great **Tar Heel** for driver Del Cameron and trainer Delvin Miller won in 2:00 flat, making him the first three-year-old to achieve that milestone.

In 1951 one of the greatest sires, **Tar Heel,** was victorious with Del Cameron. In 1952 **Meadow Rice** won with T. Wayne Smart. In 1953 it was **Keystoner** with Frank Ervin in the bike, and in 1954 **Adios Harry** with Morris MacDonald was the victor. The 1955 Jug was won by **Quick Chief** which would be Bill Haughton's first of many Jug wins.

The Little Brown Jug quickly grew. In 1956 The Jug provided the anchor for The Triple Crown of Pacing to go along with The Cane Pace at Yonkers Raceway in New York and The Messenger Stake, then held at Roosevelt Raceway in Westbury, N.Y.

Noble Adios was the winner in 1956 for John Simpson, Sr. and in 1957 the brilliant **Torpid** gave Simpson back-to-back wins.

In 1958 **Shadow Wave** with 'Jigglin' Joe O'Brien won the $65,252 purse and in 1959 the great **Adios Butler** with the power team of Clint Hodgins and Paige West broke the 2:00 barrier with a 1:59.2 clocking, becoming the first Triple Crown Winner.

THE 60s

In the 60s the sub 2:00 minute miles would continue with **Bullet Hanover** and John Simpson winning the 1960 Jug in 1:59 3/5.

In 1961 **Henry T. Adios** with Stanley Dancer won for owners Dr. & Mrs. Nicholas Derrico, and the 1962 Jug was won by **Lehigh Hanover**, again with Dancer in a time of 1:59.3.

In 1963 the great **Overtrick** with trainer/driver John Patterson Sr. won in a sizzling 1:57.3 besting *Country Don* and *Meadow Skipper*; and in 1964 Haughton was victorious with the Torpid colt, **Vicar Hanover**.

The marvelous **Bret Hanover** won for Frank Ervin in a record of 1:57 and 1: 57.2 over a track dulled by rain in 1965.

Romeo Hanover won in 1966 for driver George Sholty and trainer Jerry Silverman. In 1967 **Best Of All** won for James Hackett.

The very first Little Brown Jug I called was in 1968. It was a strong field of pacers with contenders *Rum Customer, Adios Waverly, Bye Bye Pat, Batman* and *Bye and Large.*

Rum Customer with the great Billy Haughton won the final in 1:59.3 bringing home the first six-figure purse of $104,226.

In 1969 it was **Laverne Hanover**, again with Haughton. *Lightning Wave* and Marc Ferguson won the first division in 2:00.2 and the final by **Laverne Hanover** in 2:00.2.

<u>THE 70s</u>

The 70s would speed up the timer where almost all Jug winners went faster than 2:00 as the purses continued to soar.

Another thrilling Jug was when driver Roland Beaulieu was asked if he knew 'that if he was going to win The Jug with his horse **Columbia George** it would most likely take three heats to do it.' So he brought the horse out for the first time to the track before 9 a.m.

After jogging two miles he brought **Columbia George** back to the barn, only to return to the track around 10:30. At noon he was back going a slow mile of 2:25 and at 1:30 he went a mile in 2:20.

The poor horse had been on the track four times in 4½ hours before the first heat even took place!

In the final *Columbia George* was cutting the mile as driver Curly Smart with *Leander Lobell* was hung every step of the mile.

If Roland would have just been patient he would have won The Jug but he got excited and tapped George. The horse took off, allowing Dancer and *Most Happy Fella* to get out and win the race.

Most Happy Fella won the first heat while *Columbia George* the trailer in a field of 11 came flying at the end to finish third. The next heat with a much favorable position, *Columbia George* was victorious.

Most Happy Fella would win the final, setting an all-time three-heat world record, which was the onset of The Meadow Skipper Era.

In my opinion that was one of the most exciting Jugs ever. The win by **Most Happy Fella** put him on his way to being a Triple Crown Champion.

1971 was probably one of the biggest Jug upsets ever when **Nansemond** with Herve Fillion defeated the brilliant *Albatross.*

H T Luca with Del Insko won the first division, *Albatross* took the second division and **Nansemond** won the second heat. The three winners returned for the third heat which was won by **Nansemond** in 2:04.2---last half in 1:01.1—last ¼ in 28 flat.

The 1972 Jug was won by Keith Waples with the Bret Hanovers' first crop son, **Strike Out**. The USTA film that year began with Owner/Trainer John Hayes Sr. saying, *"I didn't come to Ohio to be elected Governor, I came to win The Little Brown Jug."*

In 1973 **Melvin's Woe**, another Bret Hanover, prevailed for Trainer/Driver Joe O'Brien.

(Not sure if you knew that **Melvin's Woe** was horse-napped from a pasture field in Ohio following the The Jug, only to be returned later.)

Armbro Omaha would be victorious for Haughton and J. Elgin Armstrong in 1974 and the Meadow Skipper gelding, **Seatrain,** would win in 1975 for driver Benny Webster in 1:59.4 becoming the first gelding to win The Little Brown Jug.

On the morning of the draw Hank came to me and asked how many horses were in the Jug? I replied "19." He said he only had 18 and wanted to know what horse he was missing. It was the eventual winner, **Seatrain.**

Dancer would be first to finish with **Keystone Ore** in 1976 and **Governor Skipper** with John Chapman driving for trainer Buck Norris won the 1977 Jug in 1:56.

When the caretaker took the morning feed to **Governor Skipper** he discovered a two-inch splinter lodged in the horse's gum. Since they couldn't treat him, trainer Norris changed his bit to a rubber one so it wouldn't agitate the horse's mouth. It worked, for he won.

In 1978 it would be **Happy Escort** for trainer/driver Bill Popfinger in a race-off in 2:00.4, becoming Most Happy Fella's first Jug winner. **Happy Escort** was owned by Robert Suslow. During the winners' circle interview, I discovered this was the first horse Suslow ever owned. Talk about being blessed by the racing Gods!

When I ran into Mr. Suslow in The Log Cabin afterwards I congratulated him again. Later that year I received a small box in the mail containing a beautiful gold Jug charm, which I later purchased a gold chain to hang it on.

I bought the chain from my jeweler in Xenia for $12. (This was well before my affinity for rings) The jeweler, Donnie Coates, asked me what the chain was for. When I showed him the charm he replied, *"No Roger, you want the chain that costs $109.99."*

The gold Little Brown Jug charm was 24 karat solid gold and deserved to be hung on an expensive chain. (By the way---Mr. Suslow was the Chairman of the Board of Saks Fifth Avenue.)

Strike Out's son, **Hot Hitter**, would win the final Jug of the 70s for Herve Filion in a record time of 1:55.3. That was the year Filion returned to the winner's circle standing on **Hot Hitter 's** sulky seat--- a remarkable feat, as well as when he won The Adios.

THE 80s

Starting in the 80s the superstar **Niatross** would win the 1980 Jug for Clint Galbraith in a record time of 1:54.4. (Remember this was almost 40 years ago, so that time was phenomenal) However, I, and many others felt **Niatross** could have gone much faster if he had been challenged.)

The only filly to ever win a Little Brown Jug was the great **Fan Hanover.** She won the 1981 Jug for driver Glen Garnsey. There was an accident that year, but lucky for **Fan Hanover**, Garnsey had her out and moving three-wide down the backside when the accident took place on the inside; thus avoiding the incident.

In 1982 **Merger,** another son of Albatross with John Campbell driving was victorious, taking the majority of the $328,900 purse.

In 1983 **Ralph Hanover** with Ron Waples won The Jug in 1:55.3, and in 1984 **Colt Fortysix** with trainer/driver Chris Boring won in 1:55.2. I have always felt that the best horse in that race was *Legal Notice* with Dr. John Hayes Jr. who got buried in the two-hole and never saw the light of day.

In 1985 Niatross' greatest son **Nihilator** got up in the final stride for driver Billy O'Donnell and trainer Haughton, lowering the record-breaking time of 1:52.1.

The 1986 Jug would be won by **Barberry Spur** for Meadows hometown trainer Richard Stillings and owner Roy Davis and Barberry Farms in 1:54. Billy O'Donnell was in the sulky.

1987 was a repeat victory for the hometown team, but this time Richard Stillings was in the bike for brother Buddy, the trainer. The brothers would win the Jug with **Jaguar Spur** in 1:54 and 1:55.3.

In 1988, **B J Scoot** with the combo of Mike Lachance and Tom Artandi won in 1:52.3 for a purse of $486,050. The team of LaChance and Artandi would come back and win the next year in 1989 with **Goalie Jeff**. It was the highest purse to date of $500,200. This was a race that stands out in my mind because during the race I noticed Mike Lachance sitting directly behind the horse in front of him, giving *Goalie Jeff* cover.

The moment I saw Lachance go to the outside of the drivers shoulder I yelled, *"Mike Lachance must go NOW"*, thus I called him out before his actual move.

That night at the after-party one of the owners of The Centre Ice Stable (Owner of Goalie Jeff) came over and thanked me for telling Mike when to pull.

<u>THE 90s</u>

The 90s Jugs would pay winners over a half-million dollars in purses starting in 1990 with **Beach Towel** for trainer Larry Remmen and brother, driver Ray Remmen.

Precious Bunny and *"All you gotta know is Jackie Mo"* driver Jack Moiseyev for trainer Bill Robinson won in 1991 with an incredible burst of speed in the second elimination in 1:54, and then winning the final in 1:55.

Before the race Richie Silverman (driver of *Die Laughing*) and Jack Moiseyev made a bet on who could leave the gate the fastest. When the two horses were coming off the turn into the stretch before the start, Richie tapped *Die Laughing* and the horse made a slight break slowing his momentum.

Although *Precious Bunny* was flying out of the gate, the slight bobble from *Die Laughing* made it look even faster.

Fake Left and Ron Waples were victorious in 1992 for trainer George Sholty and owner Dreamaire Stable. Earlier that day driver Mickey McNichol was involved in a mishap, thus he could not drive in the race, so Ron Waples was put up.

Life Sign won in 1993 for the team of John Campbell/Gene Riegle for Brittany Farms in a record 1:52, out gaming *Presidential Ball* and the Jate Lobell son, *Riyadh*.

In the winners circle driver John Campbell said, "it was his worst drive ever" for he was hung to the ¼ and got to the rail only to pull about 5 seconds later—thus he was parked almost every step of the mile.

In 1994 **Magical Mike** (Hey, maybe that's where they got the name for the movie?) won with Mike Lachance and trainer Tom Haughton (Bill's son) for owners Tom Walsh and David McDuffee.

This is one time I regret saying something I couldn't take back. In the winner's circle I asked Tommy Haughton about his late brother, Peter. He broke down which took the high and thrill of a victory away.

The 1995 Jug would go to **Nick's Fantasy** for Caroline Lyon, making her the first woman trainer to win The Jug. Driver John Campbell lowered the record in a time of 1:51.2 making **Nick's Fantasy** the second gelding to win The Little Brown Jug.

In 1996 **Armbro Operative** would be victorious for Jack Moiseyev with a purse of $542,240 giving owner Tom Walsh and David McDuffee their 2nd Jug winner in 3 years.

In 1997 the Western Hanover gelding, **Western Dreamer** with the team of Mike Lachance/ Bill Robinson set a record by taking one tick off the record in 1:51.1. **Western Dreamer** went on to win The Pacing Triple Crown.

Shady Character with driver Ron Pierce/ trainer Brett Pelling would take home the trophy in 1998; and ending out the decade was **Blissful Hall** winning with Ron Pierce, driving for trainer Ben Wallace. **Blissful Hall** went on to be a Triple Crown Winner.

THE 2000s

We are now into the 2000s and there will be a lot of exciting upsets and history making Jugs.

Starting in 2000, **Astreos,** driven by Canadian driver Chris Christoforou for his dad owner Chrysomilas and co-partner Banjo Farms won The Jug. The trainer was Brett Pelling and the final time was 1:55.3, after winning the elimination in 1:54.4. The owners were so happy that they gave me a matching Little Brown Jug Trophy like theirs.

In 2001 **Bettors Delight** driven by Mike Lachance edged out archrival *Real Desire* in 1:51.4. Scott McEnery trained for owner John Grant.

In 2002 **Million Dollar Cam** with Luc Quellette for trainer Bill Robinson and owner Jeffrey Snyder would lower the track record to 1:50.2.

2003 would be **No Pan Intended** with "The Buckeye" David Miller in the bike for trainer Ivan Sugg, and owner Peter Pan Stables.

In 2004 **Timesarechanging** with Ron Pierce for Brett Pelling was victorious, and the 2005 Little Brown Jug was one of my all time favorites for driver Dave Palone, who I had known even before his driving career began, won with **P-Forty Seven**. Trainer Kelly O'Donnell and his father Richard were also good friends of mine. The owners were Mark Maynard, Richard O'Donnell and Ed Mullinax.

Mr. Feelgood won in 2006 for the team of Mark McDonald and the great Jimmy Takter. It would be Takter's first Triple Crown with a pacer. The time was 1:50.3. Canamerica, Diversity Stable and Lindy Farms were the owners.

In 2007 driver Jody Jamieson would win for trainer Blair Burgess with Real Desire's son, ***Tell All.*** The time was 1:52.2 and the purse was $480,000. ***Tell All*** was owned *by My Desire Stable.*

Shadow Play with David Miller for trainer Dr. Ian Moore won in 1:50.1 in the year 2008. Lucky for the winner the great *Somebeachsomewhere* chose not to compete. (He was eligible)

In 2009 trainer Steve Elliott and driver Ron Pierce won the Jug with ***Well Said*** with that incredible third-quarter sweep in 1:51.4. I believe this is the only time a horse won a elimination from Post 8. The owners were Jeff Snyder & Lothlorien.

In 2010 once again there would be a new record when ***Rock N Roll Heavens*** avenging sire *Rocknroll Hanover* (the 2005 disappointment) with Dan Dube would stop the clock in 1:49.2 in both the elimination and final for a two-heat World Record. Frank J. Bellino was the owner.

I have never wanted a horse to win more than in 2011 for my dear friends, owners Ed and Suzie Dupler-Telle, Ron Potter and driver David Miller.

Big Bad John won The Jug in 1:50 flat. After winning the final we played the recording of Big Bad John by Jimmy Dean.

My relationship with Big Bad John continues today. I have stopped at Midland Acres in Ohio to see him and when he returned to Delaware Jug Week I would massage his gums, putting him to sleep.

That morning someone in the crowd yelled, *"What if he swallows one of Roger's rings?"* I answered, *"It will come out eventually."*

Together, Big Bad John and I were 9 for 9 during his racing career.

His owner, Suzie, tells me when he was stabled at Delaware he would go to the back of the stall and look towards the track when he heard my voice calling a race.

(Sorry Jason Settlemoir, but when you were announcing, Big Bad John would lie down and go to sleep.)

In 2012 trainer Casie Coleman would win her first of several Little Brown Jugs with the elimination and final in 1:50 with **Michaels Power** and Scott Zeron. Jeff Snyder was the owner.

It was back-to-back wins for Casie Coleman when in 2013 **Vegas Vacation** would be victorious in 1:50 flat with Brian Sears. The owners were West Win Stables, Sorella, Beaton and Saunders.

In 2014 **Limelight Beach** driven by Yannick Gingras and trainer Ron Burke won the Jug in 1:50.4. That year for the Jug the draw for Post-Positions was held on the Saturday before. My friend and part owner of Limelight Beach, Charlie Wingfield, was sitting in the Log Cabin with one of Charlie's brothers. I told Charlie that when he won The Jug the first person I would interview would be him.

The other owners were Burke Racing Stable, Weaver-Bruscemi and M1 Stable.

One of my favorite—NO--- THE most exciting Jug for me was in 2015 when Montrell Teague and **Wiggle It Jiggleit** won in 1:49.3 in an oh-so-tight photo getting up in the last stride to defeat *Lost For Words.*

The trainer was Clyde Francis, and Montrell's father George Teague was the owner. (Since this was one of my all time favorites I dedicated an entire chapter (11) to the horse and the Teagues.)

In 2016 **Betting Line** made it three Jug winners for trainer Casie Coleman with David Miller driving, in 1:49 flat—setting a new record. The owners were West Win Stable, Christine Calhoun and MacNichol.

The *Somebeachsomewhere* colt, **Filibuster Hanover** with driver Yannick Gingras for trainer Ron Burke won in 1:50 in 2017 for owners Burke Racing Stable, J. DiScala, T. Silva, and Weaver-Bruscemi.

In 2018 the Art Major colt, **Courtly Choice** with David Miller won in 1:49.4 with a purse of $642,000. The trainer was Blake Macintosh and the owners were Hutt Racing Stable, Mac & Heim Stables, Daniel Plouffe and Touch Stone Farms. For part owner Daniel Plouffe, it was his second Jug win, having owned Blissful Hall.

I've had the honor of calling The Little Brown Jug for 51 years. Some may have been more exciting than others, but I guarantee each and every one meant something very special to me.

I hope to be able to continue calling the races at The Little Brown Jug as long as the good Lord will allow. The races are going faster, the purses are increasing, and the fans are as enthusiastic as the very first one I called.

After all, Jug Day always held the third Thursday in September after Labor Day is virtually a regional holiday in Central Ohio.

Yes, The Little Brown Jug has emerged as Harness Racing's most attended Super Bowl type event and I'm honored to be known as, "The Voice of the Jug."

A little more interesting information on The Jug:

The most wins by a driver: A 3 way tie.
Billy Haughton had 5 (1955. 1964, 1968, 1969, 1974)
Mike Lachance had 5 (1988, 1989, 1994, 1997, 2001)
David Miller had 5 (2003, 2008, 2011, 2016, 2018)

The most wins by a trainer:
Billy Haughton had 6 (1955, 1964, 1968, 1969, 1974, 1985)

Stakes Record
Betting Line 1:49

Barry Vicroy presenting me The Voice Podium

Ohio Harness Racing Wall of Fame
Scioto Downs Clubhouse
2002

Bruce and Sabrina Trogdon
Fear The Dragon win The Adios
2017

Adios' Orchards

The broodmare barn at Meadow Lands Farm.

Adios hits a pace with owner Delvin Miller up during a morning workout.

Delvin Miller and Adios

CHAPTER EIGHT

The Adios: The Pace for the Orchids

As I said in Chapter 6 the most prestigious race held at The Meadows Racetrack is **The Delvin Miller Adios: The Pace For the Orchids.**

There are several historical events I believe should be noted, such as: 1972 was the only time the Adios Pace race final (which was later renamed The Delvin Miller Adios Pace) ended in a dead heat. The horses were **Strike Out** & **Jay Time**.

In 1985 **Nihilator** and **Marauder** won the first two heats of The Adios Pace. However, in the race off *Nihilator* was scratched and it was a walk over for *Marauder* and *Dick Richardson* in a time of 2:27.2.

Marauder was the best racing son of *Sonsam,* but unfortunately not much in the breeding shed.

1997 was the only year there was a disqualification when the horse *Dream Away* finished first by five lengths, but was disqualified for interference. Dan Ross was placed the winner with **Legacy of Power.**

I asked Vicki if she thought it would be too much and bore the reader if we went into detail on the horses and the years of the Adios'. She thought it would be something you would want to know about, so if you find it a bit too much, you can blame her! Lol.

I will be writing about certain Adios' that were extra special to me either because of hometown owners, drivers, or trainers; or something extraordinary that happened in that race.

****

The very first Adios was held in 1967. It was won by **Romulus Hanover** and driver Billy Haughton. *Romulus* was almost scratched from the final because of a calcium deposit on his left front leg, but Haughton decided to let him race, thus he maneuvered *Best of All* in 2:00.3 with a purse of $85,510.

Romulus Hanover was a great colt, although he was hard to keep sound. His dam *Romalie Hanover* was arguably the greatest pacing broodmare in history and his full brother was the champion *Romeo Hanover*. Unfortunately, he too failed in the breeding shed.

The next year in 1968, Haughton had an entry: **Bye and Large** and *Rum Customer*. Haughton drove *Rum Customer* and put George Sholty up on stablemate, **Bye and Large** -- obviously thinking the colt was the weaker of the two.

Haughton guessed wrong as **Bye and Large** won both heats. The time was 2:00.1 and the purse was $93,320. **Bye and Large** was by *Bye Bye Byrd* out of an Adios dam, *Miracle Adios*. Like *Romulus Hanover,* he also was a better racehorse than sire.

1969 would have **Laverne Hanover** take home the orchids and a purse of $88,970 for owner Thomas Murphy Jr. Billy Haughton was back in the winners' circle, but not without incident. **Laverne Hanover** was the favorite in the first heat, but after Haughton tapped him in the stretch the colt broke stride and finished last.

Laverne came back to win the second heat and was victorious in the race off with *Kat Byrd*. The time was 2:01. The winner, driven and trained by Billy Haughton would make it "three in a row" at The Meadows for Haughton as a trainer.

Laverne Hanover was retired to stud at the end of the 1971 race season, having won 61 of his 98 career starts.

THE 70s

In 1970 ***Most Happy Fella*** and *Columbia George* won the two heats of the Adios and were ordered back for a race off. ***Most Happy Fella,*** with trainer/ driver Stanley Dancer was victorious in 2:19.1, last ¼ in 31 seconds. Owner Egyptian Acres Stable was awarded the winner's share of the $86,740 purse.

Rumor had it that since the race was on live television and it was almost 11 p.m., when *Columbia George* had broke a hobble hanger driver Beaulieu tied a knot in the hanger instead of replacing it. He said it wouldn't make a difference.

Most Happy Fella was a big, rugged looking colt but was somewhat rough-gaited. His driver Stanley Dancer said, "*What a nasty horse he was to drive. You never knew when he was going to break.*" But that didn't stop the horse from being one of the greatest sires in history, totally extending and embellishing the Meadow Skipper line.

1971 the great ***Albatros****s*, again for trainer/ driver Stanley Dancer, won the first heat in 1:58.3. In the second heat it was ***Albatross*** again, this time winning in 1:59.3 and setting a stake record in the combined time for owners, *Amicable Stable*. The purse was $88,800.

Albatross went on to win $1,2011,477 in his career, but really made his mark as a sire. His sons and daughters won $130,700,280 and he was voted "Horse of the Year" in 1971 and 1972.

In 1972 **Strike Out** with Keith Waples driving for trainer John Hayes Sr. dead heated with *Jay Time* and driver/trainer Gene Riegle in 1:58.1 This was one of the few dead heats in racing history of a major stake race and the 'only' one in the Adios. The purse of $92,110 was split between owners Beejay Stable & Mr. & Mrs. Carl Bass.

Before retiring to stud, **Strike Out** barely struck out in his racing career compiling a 29-9-1 record in 44 starts before retiring to stud In Kentucky.

Ricci Reenie Time went into the Adios winless for the year but ended up breaking that streak by winning the 1973 Adios for trainer/driver Harold Dancer Jr. in a time of 2:00.2 and a purse of $86,780.

In 1974 **Armbro Omaha** won for trainer/driver Billy Haughton and owners Armstrong Brothers in 1:58. The purse was $104,350. That year was the closest Delvin Miller came to winning The Adios, as he was beaten a neck with *Tarport Low* in the final.

The 1975 Adios was won *by* **Nero** in 1:57.3. In the first heat, **Nero** won in an impressive 1:58.3, while his rival *Whata Baron* and Lew Williams captured the second division in the time of 1:57.2.

Nero's driver was Jigglin Joe O'Brien, who was also the trainer. The owners were R. Derveas Jr, J. Massau, J. Crane and Stoner Creek Stud. The purse was $111,645.

The first Adios I announced was in 1976 and was a dandy.

Armbro Ranger with Joe O'Brien won the first division in 1:56.3. The owner was J. Elgin Armstrong for a purse of $128,663. Stanley Dancer and *Keystone Ore* won the second division in a world record of 1:56, and **Armbro Ranger** won the 2nd heat final, equaling the world record of 1:56.

Earlier that year owner J. Elgin Armstrong sent two modified sulkies to Joe O'Brien who didn't like them. Joe never took them out of the boxes.

1977 **Governor Skipper** with John Chapman didn't let the world record stand very long winning the first division in 1:54.4!

Nat Lobell won the second division in 1:56, but **Governor Skipper** took the final heat in 1:56.3 in a hard fought stretch duel. The trainer was Bucky Norris, the owner was Ivanhoe Stable, and the purse was $120,450.

Governor Skipper, a son of *Meadow Skipper* went on to win the Messenger with driver John Chapman who said, *"He's the best three-year-old I've ever driven."*

The owner of the Ivanhoe Stable was William Wertz who also owned The Chicago Black Hawks hockey team.

The 1978 Adios was won by **Abercrombie** in the time of 1:55. Trainer/driver Glen Garnsey got the job done for owners L. Keith Bulen & Shirley Mitchell. The purse was $128,663.

In the Winners Circle driver Glen Garnsey said, *"It was the biggest thrill ever, winning the Adios because of my respect for Delvin Miller and The Adios."* **Abercrombie** went on to be one of the sport's leading sires.

The 70s Adios ended with ***Hot Hitter*** winning for Herve Filion. It had been raining and the track was very muddy. The favorite going into the race was the unbeatable colt, *Sonsam*.

Hot Hitter and Herve won the first heat in 1:56.3 as *Sonsam* was locked in on the rail. In the second heat *Sonsam* broke stride, tried to make up ground, but couldn't catch ***Hot Hitter.***

The trainer was Louis Meittinis and the owners were Alterman Stables, SAJ Ranch and Ltd./Solomon Katz. The time was 1:57 and the purse was $150,000.

The 1979 Adios was probably the most memorable one in history because after winning the race driver Herve Filion returned to the stands standing in the sulky seat. The crowd went wild seeing a sight they had never seen before.

Herve was one of the best drivers and nicest men I knew. His legacy will be held forever by this incredible feat, although The Meadows Dave Palone would also perform this unbelievable accomplishment on the occasion of scoring win number 15,181 surpassing Herve Filion, who was humbly waiting in the winners circle to congratulate him. That's the type of man Herve was: a sportsman and true gentleman.

THE 80s

The horse that won the 1980 Adios was foaled the exact time a tornado hit the area of Castleton Farm at Lexington, Kentucky.

Thus, they named the new foal ***Storm Damage****.*

In 1980 ***Storm Damage*** won The Adios with Joe O'Brien for trainer Jerry Smith who co-owned him with his wife Betty Smith, along with Castleton Farm.

The time was 1:53.2 and the purse was $150,000. O'Brien won his third and final Adios with **Storm Damage** and set a world record.

USTA Photographer George Smallsreed reported that the picture of **Storm Damage** coming home was the first ever taken of a horse with all four hooves above the axel of the race bike.

In 1981, **Landslide**, a colt who only competed in two races before racing in the Adios surprised the fans by winning both heats in 1:56.1 and 1:57.2 over a sloppy track.

Trainer/driver Eddie Lohmeyer and co-owner Landslide Stable won the richest Adios to date with a purse of $155,000.

Higher Power, a little unassuming colt won in 1982 with Mickey McNichol driving for trainer Ron Gurfein. Sent off at 27 to 1 the colt roared through the stretch to overtake *Merger* to win in 1:54 flat. The purse was $206,000 for owners Pearl Katz and Peter Rhulen.

In 1983 **Ralph Hanover** was victorious for driver Ron Waples and Stewart Firlotte. He tallied straight wins in 1:56 and 1:54.4. It was the highest purse ever of $242,000 for owners Waples, Pointsett Stables & Grants Direct Stables.

Ralph Hanover won the 1983 Triple Crown capturing The Messenger Stakes, The Cane Pace and The Little Brown Jug. He was syndicated for $7 million, but unfortunately was not as successful as a sire.

The 1984 Adios was the first of the modern day Adios races contested at night. **Andre***l* won in 1984 with John Campbell in the bike. Trainer and owner was James Crane with a purse of $250,586 and the time was 1:54.2.

In 1985 the great *Nihilator* was the heavy favorite going into the Adios, but a horse named **Marauder** had something to say about that. Driven by trainer/driver Dick Richardson, **Marauder** tied the world record of 1:52.1.

Nihilator and Bill O'Donnell won the second heat but did not come back for the final so **Maraude***r* was declared the winner of The Adios after a walkover in 2:27.2.

Nihilator was the first Standardbred racehorse to win $3 million at the time of his retirement. He was a star and was treated as such by having his own vet, Dr. Kenneth Seeber; was shipped in a Woodbury Horse Trailer all by himself and even had a song written about him. *Nihilator* had not one by two caretakers—Gloria Stevenson and Chuck Roback.

Up until then no local horse ever won the Adios. In 1986 hometown favorite **Barberry Spur** for trainer/driver Dick Stillings broke that streak. The owners were locals Roy Davis & Barberry Farms of Sewickley, Pa.

Barberry Spur won the first heat in 1:53.3. Division two went to *Tylers Mark* and John Campbell. In the final **Barberry Spur** was victorious, making the winners' circle one of the largest in the history of the track. The final heat was 1:53.1 and the purse was $233,450.

In 1987 the Meadows home team of Stillings, Davis and Barberry Farm*s* was hoping to make it two in a row with *Jaguar Spur. Jaguar* won the fist division in 1:53.2, but in division two, **Run The Table** cruised to victory in 1:54 and crossed the finish line first in the final heat for brothers John Campbell in the bike and trainer Jim Campbell. The owners were Dalona Stables, the time was 1:53 .2 and the purse $240,076.

In the 1988 Adios there were 2 divisions--- carrying the highest purse ever. *Dare To You* and John Campbell won the first division.

Camtastic won the second division in 1:54.2 while the third division went to *Albert Albert* in 1:53.3.

Camtastic roared out of the gate and won the second heat in 1:53.3 for Billy Haughton. Bob Bencal was the trainer for owner Dreamaire Stable Corp. and the purse was $277,055.

Closing out the eighties was **Goalie Jeff**, the son of *Cam Fella*. The Stillings brothers had entered *Kentucky Spur* and despite a foot problem won the second heat in 1:55.2.

Mike Lachance was in the sulky for trainer Tom Artandi as **Goalie Jeff** won the final in 1:54.2. The owner was Centre Ice Stable and the purse was $275,045.

THE 90s

The 1990 Adios was a little 'iffy' because of something I said to Ray Remmen about The North American Cup. I commented that he had his horse *Beach Towel* so confused going to the quarter by leaving, taking a hold, then going forward that he made a slight break.

When I saw Remmen at The Meadowlands and invited him and **Beach Towel** to the Adios he replied, *"I'm not coming because you tore into me in Canada."* Of course he was joshing and entered **Beach Towel** in the race.

Beach Towel won the Adios in a time of 1:51.4 for brothers Ray Remmen (driver) and Larry Remmen (trainer). The purse of $493,176 was the highest ever. Uptown Stable was the owner.

The owner, Seth Rosenfeld, was a good friend as he and his mother Lana always spent the night when racing at The Meadows with me in the Announcers Booth.

1991 was the Silver Anniversary for the Adios.

Artsplace and **Precious Bunny** were the morning line favorites. In the first division, *Artsplace* defeated **Precious Bunny** in a world record: equaling the time of 1:50.4.

In the second division *Three Wizards* and Bill Gale defeated *Nuke of Earl* in 1:54.3. In the final, Jack Moiseyev and **Precious Bunny** prevailed in 1:50.4.

The trainer was Bill Robinson, the owner was R. Peter Heffering and the purse was $428,880.

Direct Flight won in 1992 for driver John Campbell and trainer Kelvin Harrison in 1:53.4. The owner was Joe Aflen and the purse was $256,308.

The 1993 Adios was won by **Miles McCool** in 1:51.2 for driver John Campbell and trainer Tommy Haughton. In the second division, *Riyadh* set a world record in 1:50.1. Afterwards, Riyadh's driver Jim Morrill said he thought his horse could have gone in 1:48 if he was pressured.

The other division was won by *Mystical Prince* and Ron Pierce in 1:51.5. In the final, *Riyadh* was sitting third; however, *Mystical Prince* who was on the front jumped a shadow causing confusion at the ¾ pole. Campbell would win the race for owner Joe Alflen. The purse was $254,160. This was the second Adios win for owner Joe Aflen.

The 1994 Adios was won by **Cam's Card Shark**. In the first division *Cam* won in 1:50.4 and in the second the winner *Historic* with Doug Brown upset *Magical Mike* and Jack Moiseyev in 1:51 flat. In the final, *Magical Mike* made a break in the first turn, allowing **Cam's Card** Shark to be victorious in 1:51.1.

Once again John Campbell was in the sulky making it 'three in a row.' Bill Robinson was the trainer and the owner was Jeffrey Snyder. The purse was $256, 512.

In 1995 **David's Pass**, again with John Campbell, won in 1:51.4. Unfortunately this year the locals would not be victorious. The No Nukes son *Neutrality* (co-owned by author Vicki Howard) finished second to **David's Pass** in both the first heat and final. *Nick's Fantasy* driven by Bob Ritchie won the second division and showed in the final.

The trainer for the winner was Brett Pelling and the owner was RJS Stable. The purse was $264,768.

After the race driver Bob Ritchie asked John Campbell if he had a drive in The Jug and if he didn't would he handle *Nick's Fantasy*. The answer was, *"He didn't have a drive and yes he would love to drive Nick's Fantasy."* Campbell and *Nick's Fantasy* went on to win The Jug a month later.

Electric Yankee with Mike Lachance won the 1996 Adios in 1:52.1 for winning trainer Brett Pelling. This would be Pelling's second Adios win in a row.

The owner was Charlie Keller and the purse was $163,852.

In 1997 **Legacy Power** was placed the winner for local driver Dan Ross and his father, trainer Jerry Ross Sr. in a time of 1:52.1 with a purse of $196,248. *Dream Away* had won the final but was disqualified for interference.

Artist Stena won the 1998 Adios with driver Luc Quelette and 'down under' trainer Ross Croghan. The time was 1:51.1 and the purse was $200,000. Ecurie Stena was the proud owner.

Ending the decade was Meadows leading driver Dave Palone winning the 1999 Adios with **Washington VC**. The trainer was Ronald Coyne and the owner was Richard Bolte. The time was 1:52.3 and the purse was $284,331.

Co-host Jerry Erenstein correctly picked Palone to win the final feeling that due to track bias Palone would have **Washington VC** in a spot to come home three wide around the final turn---- and win he did.

In 2000 **Riverboat King** was victorious for driver Mark Kesmodel and trainer Steve Elliott in 1:51.4.

    Ain't No Stopn Him won the first elimination in 1:51.4. Division two went to *Life's Not Fair*. The owner of **Riverboat King** was The Golden Touch Stable and the purse was $257,115.

In 2001 **Pine Valley** won for local connections Brian Sears and trainer David Knight. The owners were Ed Franz, John Knight and Daniel Miller. The time was 1:51.4 and the purse was $272,547.

Million Dollar Cam, the son of *Cam's Card Shark* won the 2002 Adios in 1:50.4. *Monsoon Hall* won the first division and the second division was won by *Soho* with Richie Silverman in 1:50.2.

The driver for **Million Dollar Cam** was John Campbell and the trainer was Bill Robinson. The owners were Jeffrey Snyder and Peter Heffering. The purse was $300,000.

In 2003 **Armbro Animate** won for driver John Campbell and his brother trainer Jim in 1:52.2. The owners were Arlene & Jules Siegel and the purse was $265,416.

Iced Yankee and David Miller won the first division in 1:52 and *General* Challenge and Dave Palone won the second division.

The 2004 Adios was won **by *Timesarechanging*** with Ron Pierce in the sulky. *Georgia Pacific* and Brian Sears won the first division. Locally owned and trained *Basil Hanover* won the second division in 1:50.3 for driver Mike Wilder.

Timesarechanging won the third division and the final, drawing away by two lengths. The trainer was Brett Pelling and the owner was Perfect World Enterprises. The time was a new record of 1:49.3 and the purse was $350,350.

Village Jolt took home the orchids and a purse of $321,800 in 2005. The team of Ron Pierce/Brett Pelling won their second Adios in a row in a time in 1:52.1. The owners were Jeffrey Snyder and Arlene & Jules Siegel. It was the fourth Adios victory for trainer Brett Pelling.

In 2006 **Cactus Creek**, a 20 to 1 shot was victorious for driver Mike Lachance and trainer Erv Miller. The time was 1:50.2 and the purse was $300,000. The owners were Brittany Farm*s* and Stanley Friedman.

The 2007 Adios was very special for locals and one that trainer Mickey Burke will never forget. The 71-year-old trainer had never won a 'Pace For The Orchids' at his home track before.

With George Brennan in the bike, **May June Character** won in 1:51. Burke also had two stable mates, *Won The West* and *Pan Giovanni* who finished a respective second and third. The Burke Stable swept the board finishing first, second, and third. The owners of **May June Character** were Sandy Goldfarb & A Bunch of Characters II and the purse was $320,125.

In 2008 **Shadow Play** set a world record of 1:48.2 in his elimination, then won the final in 1:50.4.

David Miller was the driver for trainer Mark Ford.

Dr. Ian Moore, Serge Savard and R G McGroup were the owners and the purse was $350,000. That year the 2008 Adios was held at Pocono Downs as The Meadows was in the process of building our Racino.

Shadow Play went on to be a great sire.

In 2009 **Vintage Master**, a 13-1 long shot and driver Dan Dube win for trainer Jimmy Takter. The time was 1:49.2 and the purse was $500,000 for owners Brittany Farms & the Estate of Brian Monieson.

In the 2010 Adios final at the finish line six horses were stretched across the track in less than a length and a half, while Ray Paver with *Trick Man* finished seventh, climbing over Brian Sears at the finish.

The winner **Delmarvelous** was owned by the Teagues; along with Badlands Racing, Elmer Fannin and Howard Dorfman. Going a grueling three quarters in 1:20.3, 17 to 1 **Delmarvelous** dug in to be victorious. The purse was $500,000. **Delmarvelous** with Brian Sears won in 1:49.4 for trainer George Teague, Jr.

The 2011 Adios was won by **Alsace Hanover** for Ron Pierce and trainer Tony O'Sullivan. In his elimination, **Alsace Hanover** set a world record for three-year-old geldings. He won the final in the fastest time ever paced by a sophomore gelding on a 5/8's mile track. The time was 1:48.3 and the purse was $500,000. The owner was John Fielding.

A world record would be set in 2012 with **Bolt The Duer** and driver Mark MacDonald. Trainer Peter Foley and owners All Star Racing took home the orchids with a purse of $500,000. The time was the fastest ever, in a blazing 1:47.4.

The next year, at age four, **Bolt The Duer** won again making him (at that time) the first horse in harness racing history to record wins in 2 times in sub- 1:48 over a 5/8's mile track.

In 2013 **Sunfire Blue Chip** with Yannick Gingras and Hall-Of-Fame trainer Jimmy Takter crossed the line first in 1:48.3. The purse was $500,000 and the owners were Jimmy's wife, Christina Takter and Jim and John Fielding.

In 2014 the great **McWicked** and David Miller won in 1:49.1 for Casie Coleman, the first female trainer to ever win an Adios final. SSG Stables was the owner and the purse was $400,000.

During the 2015 Adios, **Dudes The Man** skipped shadows most of the mile, but when coming for home a cloud blocked the sun. Driver Corey Callahan commented, "*Someone was looking out for me in the last turn.*"

 Dude's The Man was victorious for trainer Jessica Okusko in 1:48.4. The purse was $400,000 and the owners' were M&L of Delaware & Victoria Dickinson.

The 2016 Adios was the 50th edition of 'The Pace for the Orchids'. It had been raining all day and the track was listed sloppy. **Racing Hill** gave driver Brett Miller and trainer Tony Alagna their first Adios win.

 Alarmed by the brutal fractions in the first half of 25.2/52.1, Miller thought it was over for his horse. "*When I saw the time flash up, I wanted to throw up.*"

 But **Racing Hill** crossed the line first in a time of 1:48.4. The purse was $400,000 and the owner was Tom Hill.

Fear The Dragon won the Adios in 2017 in a time of 1:49.1 with driver David Miller and trainer Brian Brown for owners Bruce and Sabrina Trogdon.

 Fear The Dragon beat his stable mate, *Downbytheseaside,* winning the $1 million Pepsi North America Cup earlier in the year.

The rest of the story was that Trogdon skipped putting his horse **Fear The Dragon** in The Meadowlands Pace to race in The Adios. The reason was that in 1976 (my first year at The Meadows) Trogdon proposed to his wife Sabrina on Adios Day.

Since then The Adios was always a race they wanted to win, and they did.

In 2018 **Dorsoduro Hanover** with driver Matt Kakaley and trainer Ron Burke took home the purse of $400,000 and the orchids in a scorching 1:50.1. The owners were locals Burke Racing Stable, Silva-Purnell and Libby, Weaver-Bruscemi and Wingfield Five.

****

I have called 43 Adios'. They all were special to me in one way or another. It was good to see hometown boys such as The Stilling Brothers (Richard and Buddy), driver Dave Palone, the Burke family (Mickey Sr. and sons Ron and Mickey Jr.), Roy Davis and David Knight win the prestigious race.

Hats off to Delvin Miller and his Champion sire, Adios, for leaving a legacy at the Meadowlands, Pa. I'm sure he is looking down and smiling at each and every Adios.

ADIOS RECORDS

The Fastest

2012 1:47.4 Bolt The Duer (World Record)

Most Wins By A Driver

8 Wins John Campbell

(1984, 1987, 1992, 1993, 1994, 1995, 2002, 2003)

Most Wins By A Trainer

4 Wins Brett Pelling

(1995,1996, 2004, 2005)

Other Notable Events

In 1972 The race final was the only time the Adios Pace ended in a dead heat.

In 1997 This year the only disqualification took place in the race's history when the horse *Dream Away* finished first by five lengths, but was disqualified for interference.

Wearing the 'Be There' T-Shirt

*Bill Lowe, former Fair Manager at Delaware County Fair
and my replacement at Wilmington College*

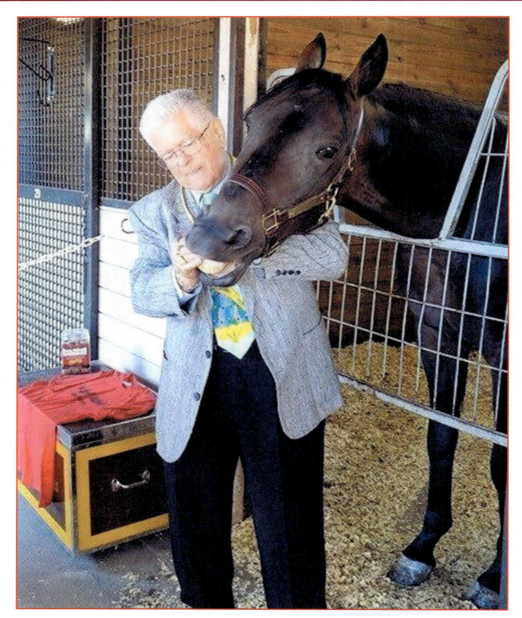

Big Bad John Loves His Gums Rubbed
2015

Darren Owen, the Top Commentator in Europe
Delaware

Delaware County Fair

Actor James Stewart
Indiana, Pa. on his 75th Birthday

CHAPTER NINE

The County Fairs

I can't stress enough how important the County Fairs have been in my life and what a big part they played.

I began going to the fairs when I was four-years-old, accompanied by my parents, Cecil and Irene. I enjoyed watching those athletic, majestic animals go around the oval track at such a fast speed. I often wondered how there weren't more accidents, for they came so close to one another; yet luckily there were very few mishaps.

I attended the Greene County Fair where I learned how to mimic the announcer calling the races. I went to Lebanon Raceway with Uncle Don when I was eleven-years-old and was mesmerized as he announced the races so effortlessly, wondering how someone could remember all the horses and drivers names in such a short time.

In the 50s my friend Fremont Whittington and I started going to The Little Brown Jug in Delaware, Ohio, never ever imagining I would one day be the announcer!

Yes, fairs have meant so much to me: (almost) as much as calling races at major racetracks. The fairs hold a soft spot in my heart and I'm so thankful of the time I had there and the wonderful people I met.

Early in my career I was referred to as a County Fair Announcer, something I was very proud of. A County Fair Announcer has two meanings: 1) I would never make it to the racetracks with the style of announcing I have, and 2) That my style fits that of a county fair horse race. (I prefer #2.)

There were many times I was told "to slow down" and not get so excited while calling a race, but that is like telling a two-year-old to sit in a chair for 30 minutes without moving or saying a word. IMPOSSIBLE!

But as I have aged I slowed down a degree, but when it comes to a horse race I'm just as excitable as the very first one I called.

Whenever I'm approached by someone who is thinking about becoming an announcer and ask my advice, I say, *"Just be yourself. Don't try to copy someone else's style. You must be comfortable in what you are doing."*

That's the best advice I can give.

****

In 1960 I made my debut at a Matinee race program sponsored by the local Sertoma Club in Wilmingon, Ohio. My first paid gig was at The Warren County Fair in Lebanon, which was given to me by my Uncle Don.

I must admit there were some rough moments but I survived enough that Frank Wilkins and Junior Luse of The Campaign County Fair approached me to announce the races that year at Urbana.

The schedule was Saturday, Monday and Thursday, and on Tuesday and Wednesday a double-header. My fee in those days was $25 per program.

After the races were over that Monday Junior Luse came over to me and said that The Fair Board had agreed to have Tuesday and Wednesday (the Stake Race Programs) heard on WBLY radio and Charlie Hinkle would be calling the races. I was devastated!

Junior told me I would still get paid and could even watch the races in the grandstand, but the Fair Board couldn't pass up the opportunity to be on the radio.

When I got home that night I immediately called Uncle Don and asked him what I could do. Unfortunately his answer was not what this seventeen-year-old announcer wanted to hear.

He said there was nothing I could do, for Charlie Hinkle was also from Xenia, Ohio and one of the biggest names in the sport. He tried to console me by saying to have patience for my day would come. I just didn't realize it at the time that it would be the next day.

Tuesday came and I was seated in the grandstand with the Urbana High School Band, sulking like a sour racehorse. Post time was 1:25 and looking at my watch I realized that the horses should have been on the track parading by then.

I heard my name being paged over the speakers to come to the Judges Stand. When I got there Junior Luse told me that Charlie Hinkle hadn't shown up yet. He asked me to call the horses to the track and continue calling them until Hinkle arrived.

I was ecstatic to have this opportunity. As I called the first race out I saw Charlie hot footing it across the infield. When he got to the stage he pulled a flask from his briefcase and took a few swigs. He grabbed the microphone out of my hand and said, *"I'll take over from here."*

I stood there with my mouth agape for I couldn't believe what had just happened.

Junior, who had never had a drink of alcohol in his life, grabbed the microphone from Hinkle and handed it back to me saying, *"Roger will be calling the races."*

I don't think Charlie was too happy!

That day I was asked to go to the grandstand and meet a man who wanted to meet me. The man told me he had been coming to the races for several years and that day was the first day he was "able to see a race." The gentleman was totally blind! Talk about making an impact on a young announcer.

That week two individuals from other fairs heard me announce and hired me to call the races at The Madison County Fair in London and the Butler County Fair in Hamilton. A week or so later my Uncle Don got a call from Dr. Sam Howe in Marietta wanting him to announce the races there, but because of his day job couldn't commit so he recommended me.

That first year I called 99 races and made around $400. I thought, *"What a great summer job this was going to be."* I had enrolled in nearby Wilmington College for I wanted to be a schoolteacher nine months a year and announce races during the summer months at the county fairs—thus I would have a year round schedule, doing the two things I loved to do.

In the mid 60's I met Richard Rudnicki from 'That State up North.' Excuse me--- this is not a football story so I can use the word 'Michigan'.

Richard had served as a Presiding Judge at various tracks, but on this particular occasion they needed a PJ at The Darke County Fair in Greenville, Ohio.

At that time they were racing eight programs, which were on Friday, Saturday, and Monday nights, doubleheaders on Tuesday and Wednesday and the final card on Thursday afternoon.

By the final day we all get a bit jovial, to say the least. Richard wanted to call a race and said I could be the Judge. This was accomplished and he did a hell of a great job, although his delivery was a bit different than mine and very noticeable.

In one of the races driver Jim Williamson of Cedarville, Ohio, got into a bit of a tight situation during the mile so Mr. Rudnicki wanted to speak to the young driver in the race office after the races.

In the speed office Richard and I were discussing racing in Michigan when in walks Jim Williamson. His first words were, *"Hey Rog, who in the world was that Preacher who called the 7ᵗʰ race?"*

Richard immediately spoke up replying, *"I am Reverend Rudnicki, who is also the Presiding Judge."*

By the way--- congratulations to Richard being awarded The Lifetime Achievement Award which is presented by The Michigan Harness Horesmen's Association. Each year when I go home for New Years or the County Fair and run into Jim, we always talk about this classic situation.

****

There are several stories I want to share concerning fairs that I think you'll appreciate.

The first fair story that comes to my mind is the one in the year 1960 or 1961 at The Madison County Fair in London. The racetrack did not have an outside fence around the final turn: just a huge cornfield. There was a trotter named *Ray Barnes* who was 11 or 12-years-old at the time and a bad, bad actor. He had been banned from all Ohio Racetracks for tearing up the paddocks, so the only place they could race him was at the fairs. The driver on *Ray Barnes* was a young man by the name of Cliff Albertson Jr.

Going to the ¾'s Ray was on top, but at the last minute he decided to check out the years' corn crop, so instead of making the turn, he trotted off straight into the cornfield!

I was speechless and the crowd aghast not knowing if we would ever see *Ray Barnes* or Cliff again, but lo and behold about five minutes later the horse and driver emerged from the field to finish the mile!

Cliff was yelling and screaming every word under the sun as he appeared in front of the grandstand with Cornstalks dangling off the sulky shafts and harness.

****

In the early 50s when my family and I would go to the Champaign County Fair to see the horseraces we sat up high in their mammoth Grandstand.

One particular day the announcer was Hap Shreve, who also served as Presiding Judge. I would call the races from the back row. (Thinking back we probably sat in the back so my folks wouldn't be embarrassed of my announcing.)

Little did I know that in 1960 I would be working alongside Hap at the Madison County Fair in London.

Hap was a very tall man and the Judges Stand had a low hanging roof. That night the Free-For-All Trot featured one of the best double-gaited horses of that time---the fabulous mare, *Great Pleasure*, who was trained and driven by McKinley Kirk of Washington Court House, Ohio.

Great Pleasure was a World Champion pacer and that night McKinley decided to try her on the trot. Needless to say, she won by open lengths.

When McKinley brought her back in front of the stands, Hap stooped down low and yelled at Kirk.

He said, *"McKinley, was she pacing in that mile coming home?"* Kirk replied, *"She sure was Hap."*

Great Pleasure was disqualified and placed last for pacing in a trotting mile.

At Greenville, Ohio, I had the opportunity of calling the great *Overtrick* winning The Parshall Futurity. Little did I know that the winner of the 1963 Little Brown Jug would be my introduction into announcing some of the sports all-time greatest horses. A few years later I would have the opportunity to call the famed Little Brown Jug.

****

Another highlight at Greenville was to spend time with Gene and Martha Riegle. Often after the races I would go to their home located down the backside of the track for dinner before calling the evening program.

I first met The Riegle's at Urbana, Ohio in 1961 when we had supper at the church restaurant below the grandstand prior to the evening card.

Around 1965 I was visiting the fair at Hilliard when Gene approached me and asked to borrow my driving boots, as he had only dress shoes with him.

What an honor to have a future Hall of Famer wear my boots to drive in races. I joke around and tell people, *"Gene Riegle walked in MY shoes!"*

But my most memorable night at Greenville was in 1972 when the horse *Jay Time* won The Parshall Futurity and became the first horse to go in 1:59 on a ½ mile county fair track in Ohio.

I can remember it as well as anything, seeing my good friend return to the winners' circle with tears streaming down his face.

****

In 1961 I added the fairs at Eaton, Springfield, Owensville and Plain City. Good ole' Plain City was one of the hardest tracks to announce races as there were six Oak trees and two baseball diamonds located in the infield. It was by far the worst lit track in Ohio.

The first race had a field of twelve. I was totally lost as the horses headed down the backside, and to top it off I intentionally knocked the power plug for the PA out of the electrical switch box. Luckily, the remaining races were short fields so there was no more problems the remainder of the evening.

In 1962 I added to the list Ottawa, Troy and Greenville, totaling twelve county fairs. The offers kept coming in and in1963 Circleville, Xenia, Upper Sandusky, Wooster and Dayton were added. That was the highlight: a total of seventeen county fairs.

With this many fairs I had to make a very important decision, which I believe to this day was the right one. You see, in a person's life they must make decisions from time to time that can change the course in their life. Every time I would come to a "Y" in the road, by the grace of God I seemed to choose the right path.

I received a call from Phil Mauger asking me to announce the Press Party races prior to their opening at Scioto Downs. Phil was at Toledo Raceway and unable to call the Press Party races so he thought I could do it, but the call came prior to the fairs and at that time my schedule was set for the year.

Later that summer I got a call from Bob Steele the General Manager at Scioto, wanting to meet with me. I met with Bob and found out he wanted me to be the announcer at Ohio's Showplace of Harness Racing for 100 nights. Although this would be a big move for me, I would have to drop all of my fairs. And the offer was 100 nights at $25 per night.

At this time in my career I was making $50, per session at the fairs, totaling around $5,000, which meant if I called the races at Ohio's Showplace of Harness Racing, I would be taking a 50% pay cut!

This was a no brainer for my Mother and Father didn't raise a fool. I told Bob, "*Thanks, but no thanks*" for the offer for I could make more money announcing the county fairs.

As the years went by I added many more Ohio Fairs including: Canton, Sidney, Mt. Vernon, Napolean, Delaware, Washington Court House, The Ohio State Fair, Ashland, Caldwell, Carollton, Kenton, McConnelsville, Old Washington, Lisbon, Medina, Canfield, Woodsfield, Zanesville, Cortland, Oak Harbor, Chillicothe and Jefferson, Ohio. This totaled thirty-nine fairs in Ohio: some of which were merely guest appearances.

I especially enjoyed The Ohio State Fair for it gave me the chance to meet a number of celebrities and personalities in the entertainment field.

Most of those years the race calling was done on the stage in the infield. At times, the stars of the evening shows would hang out while I was announcing. Some of those included The Osmonds, Jimmy Dean, and the great Sonny and Cher.

But my all-time favorite was a young, pretty singer from Australia who was making her first stateside tour. That girl was the one and only Olivia Newton John.

The night she appeared I was backstage when it started to rain. She was in the middle of signing autographs so I was asked to hold the umbrella for her. They didn't have to ask me twice!

The times at Ohio State Fair were some of my most enjoyable, but also the only time I "kinda" got fired. The Speed Superintendent was a man named James Schmidt who sent out the same Christmas card every year. On the card was Santa driving the sleigh with Rudolph crashing into an outhouse. The caption read, *"I said the SCHMIDT house!"*

****

The year I got into trouble was the year Gov. John J. Gilligan was riding in a coach pulled by 40 horses. Mr. Schmidt told me to announce the Governor when he was in front of the grandstand, for the crowd would boo him---which they did.

He went on to say when the coach was past the grandstand a man would walk across the track and I was to announce, *"Now crossing the track is the former Governor of Ohio—James A. Rhodes."*

He said the crowd would now cheer; and he was right again for they did!

Schmidt told me when that happens, *"Get in your car and get the hell out of town"*---which I did.

Sometime later I got a call from Jerry Kaltenbach who was the G.M. of the State Fair asking me if I was told to announce Governor Rhodes crossing the track, to which I replied 'yes.'

Needless to say Schmidt and myself did not work the Ohio State Fair after that.

****

I couldn't talk about the fairs without mentioning a lovely woman named Stella Hagemeyer of Clarksville, Ohio. Stella served as Clerk of Course at ten County Fairs in Ohio for 40 years and was Secretary-Treasurer of The H. M. Parshall Futurity at Greenville for 22 years.

In 1960 when I began my announcing at the fairs I first met Stella who would become a lifelong close friend until her death at age 96 in June 2018.

Stella and I worked hand-in-hand at so many fairs over the years. I would always arrive a couple hours early and try to help her as much as I could with getting the correct drivers and any scratches there were to make her job easier.

Each year I looked forward to seeing this great lady at the O.H.H.A. Annual Banquet, as she was so much a huge part of my life. I came to know her entire family over the years with their heavy involvement in Harness Racing, especially son Mel who was an integral part of Lebanon Raceway.

****

In 1970 I stopped at Scioto Downs to visit and help train some horses with my friend, Marc Ferguson. That day they were having qualifiers and a young man from Celina, Ohio was calling the races. He was new to the game but sounded real good. His name was Doug Ballinger.

Doug was also the caretaker of a pacer named *Katfish* who raced at Urbana. I later discovered that Doug had obtained a recording of my calling a race and played it so many times it wore out.

That year my career was peaking and in high gear. I was afraid I couldn't go from Lebanon to Ottawa in time for the first race so I contacted Doug and asked him to go to Ottawa in case I was running late.

I arrived in time for the first race after all but let Doug call the first two races before I took over. He did a great job and although I don't remember doing this, he says I gave him $5 –enough to cover his gas expenses from Celina to Ottawa.

In 1972 Doug announced a number of my fairs for I was calling Quarter Horse Racing at Pompano Park at that time.

In 1976 when I left Pompano Park to go to The Meadows, Doug began announcing all of my fairs in Ohio and did a great job!

In 1973 I took on the Ashland Fair, which was on top of Jug Week at Delaware. I would call the races at Delaware on Monday and Tuesday and drive some 60 miles to Ashland, giving me plenty of time to enjoy a 'Steak-On-A-Stick' before the races. When my friend Sam McKee began announcing I quickly gave him Ashland to call the races, which helped advance his career.

In 2018 I returned to both Greenville and Urbana for special nights and got to work with Doug Ballinger who is now 65 years old and still going strong at the fairs, and filling in for Steve Cross some evenings at Hoosier Park.

This year I did 7 fairs in Ohio and 4 in Pennsylvania, along with Woodstock, Virginia, The State Fair of West Virginia and Fryeburg, Maine.

I enjoy calling the fairs as much today as I did my very first time. They are all special to me and I hope to continue calling them until the Good Lord calls me home.

Training with Tom Wantz at Pompano Park
Florida

Winning at Delaware with Jubilee John
Defeating Paul Spears and Max Hempt
1987

CHAPTER TEN

My Driving Career

My driving career (understated) may have been short lived but nonetheless to me is one of the greatest achievements in my life. Of course you can't put me in the category of the all-time-greats: Haughton, Dancer, O'Brien and the latest superstars Palone, Miller, Campbell, Pierce, Gingras, Tetrick and Sears-- but I'm proud to have accomplished this and wouldn't trade it for the world. It made me realize just how dangerous it is for the drivers and horses: something underestimated by most people.

Fans know how dangerous racecar racing is, but very few times do you hear someone acknowledging how dangerous it is in horseracing. Our drivers deserve a lot more credit than they get for they put their lives on a thin line every time they drive in a race to entertain the fans.

I once heard a saying that is so true. *"Driving a racehorse is like dancing with a chainsaw."* Racing horses is a dangerous endeavor and nobody knows that more than the drivers themselves.

****

It all began in 1984 when I heard about the Delvin Miller CKG Billings Amateur Trot. I thought it would be a good idea to join, for every time I call a race I actually feel like I'm driving myself.

I mean, while I'm calling a race I put my entire heart and soul into it. I think as a driver should, anticipate his move before he actually moves, or realize they should have moved and didn't, thus getting buried alive.

I do feel all my experience at calling races gave me a slight edge over most amateur drivers I competed against. In those years I drove against the likes of some of the best: Paul Spears who was the chairman of Hanover Shoe Farms, executive Vice-President with the Standardbred Horse Sales Company, Director Emeritus of The Hambletonian Society and breeder of such notables as the trotting Triple Crown champion *Windsong's Legacy.*

I raced against Max and George Hempt. Max was George's father who had a racing stable in the late 1930s and 1940s. His first top horse was *Follow Me*— who happens to be the dam of *Stenographer.* When Max died, his son George took three of his fathers broodmares and started his own Standardbred breeding operation calling it Hempt Farms, which for over a half-century has sent thousands of yearlings to sales.

I drove against Ebby and Peter Gerry. The brothers were sons of the late Elbridge T. Gerry Sr., who is said to be a descendant of one of the signers of the Declaration of Independence.

The Gerry's came into the business of Harness Racing, forming a stable with some of the greatest trotters, including Hambletonian winners *Titan Hanover* (1945) and *Flirth* (1974).

I raced against Mal Burroughs, a recipient of USHWA's Lifetime Achievement Award who is a contractor, sportsman, horse owner and breeder. (His company built The Meadowlands Racetrack in New Jersey.)

Mel's claim to fame is that he is the only amateur driver to ever drive and win a Hambletonian. A great accomplishment indeed!

Burroughs owned and bred the Hambo winner, *Malabar Man.* In 1997 Burroughs took the lines and drove his colt to victory in the prestigious Hambletonian.

Malabar Man earned $2,143,903 and went on to be a great sire, siring *Power To Charm, Flirtin Miss, Pick Me Up, Reinvent, Malabar Maple* and *Funny Malentine.*

Malabar Man is also the grandsire of *Possess The Magic*---the winner of the 2006 Breeders Crown Two-Year-Old Filly Trot.

The Supergill colt was the very first foaled on Burrough's New Jersey farm and was named after Mal and his wife, Barbara. That itself is a rarity and something to be proud of.

I drove against local drivers like Bill Bercury, Jimmy Smith, Richard Davis (the son of the late Roy Davis who owned the great Spur horses) Logan Dickerson, and Jerry Kehm.

Not to brag but at one time or another I beat all of them—except for Bill Bercury.

In 1984 I drove four races with two seconds and a third for a UDRS of .361 and earned a whopping $1,849 for my owners; but for the life of me I can't remember the names of the horses I drove. It's much easier to remember the winners, which totaled 15 of 97 or 15.5% winning efforts over 13 years.

The first win is always the one a driver remembers as the most special. Mine was at The Meadows during Adios week before 7,000 cheering fans.

The horse was family owned *Lewis Lincoln*—a $4,000 claimer at the time. I defeated Kenny Ross (Kenny Ross Chevrolet) who drove a horse that had just raced in the Open Trot at Freehold.

After the race I sure got flack for although I was hitting the saddle pad coming home, the shaft of the whip came down on the horses' right rear. Despite the win I felt I overdrove as we won by a couple of lengths.

That was my only win in 4 drives that year as Bill Bercury beat me at Buffalo, Mal Burroughs at Delaware, and was a loser at Garden State Park.

1986 and 1987 were my best years with 7 wins in 30 starts, primarily with the veteran *Jubilee John*. Owners Cindi Tripp and Bart Bartholomew actually asked me to drive their horse, replacing drivers Frank Glessner and Charlie Flickinger.

In our first race at The Meadows (my first drive with *Jubilee John)* we finished a good second, but felt we could win the next start at Northfield if we drew well.

Draw well we did, getting the rail in a field of eight. Owner Roy Davis came into my office that morning and asked me about the upcoming race as his son, Richard, was also in the race driving *Bandit Spur*---a World Champion double-gaited horse.

I told Roy to tell his son Richard to "take a seat" as I was planning to go wire-to-wire. I even gave Roy the Trifecta box of: Huston, Gerry, Spears and Davis. This was the first Amateur Trot at Northfield and the last for a number of years.

Roy told me that the entire way to Northfield all he heard from his trainer and friend, Dick Stillings was that Roy's son, Richard, would win the race for fun.

Going into the first turn I was on top with *Jubilee John* when here comes Richard on the outside to challenge; but fortunately for me the challenge didn't last long for *Bandit Spur* made a break.

Then I saw Logan Dickerson. When I looked over I saw fear on his face as his horse's bit had broken. Past the half Logan drove his horse into the barn area, crashing into a brand new car!

Thank goodness no one was injured—except the once shiny Mercedes!

I went on to win the race for fun with Ebby Gerry finishing second and Paul Spears third, just as I predicted.

Later that year *Jubilee John* and I went to The Stoneboro Fair in their Open Trot, winning both heats against regular drivers.

In 1987 I drove *Jubilee John* to wins at The Meadows, Vernon Downs, Delaware and at Lexington winning the Billings Final.

I also got a call from Tony Genneccaro to drive *Sans Beauty*, a three-year-old filly pacer in the Pa. Sires Stakes races at the fairs. We were never able to get to the winners circle but in 10 starts we placed or showed in all of them. Not too shabby.

The off track highlight that year was driver John Green coming after me with his whip, after I hung him at Arden Downs at The Washington County Fair. Luckily, I was much faster then and able to escape his wrath.

****

In 1998 I had the hardest horse to drive in a three-year-old filly owned by Ed Ryan. Her name was *Arndoll* by *Arndon.*

The first drive was at Pocono where we were the trailer in the 2nd tier. The caretaker was Tom Kirwan who decided *Arndoll* wouldn't need the earplugs in that race.

We were behind the gate when *Arndoll* decided she wanted "on" the gate. She went up and over the wheel of Harvey Heller, which caused a recall.

I yelled at the starter Verne Gagnon to leave the wings of the car open, but he thought I told him to close the wings. Nearly 5/8's of a mile later I was able to get *Arndoll* pulled up, so this time I stayed close to 15 lengths off the gate.

We ended up finishing fourth and timed her in 1:56.4.

From that auspicious start we went on to win at Syracuse and Garden State Park in the identical times of 1:59.4.

Arndoll was quite a puller. Even with her earplugs in she would grab on as soon as we headed to the gate. After driving her, my arms would ache for days.

I always wore driving boots with a steel shank and would use the stirrups to get a better grip. That year my soles were so bruised I wore tennis shoes all week at Delaware.

In 1990 I drove *Armbro Expert*, another horse owned by Mr. Ryan and won at Delaware and Lexington. In the race at Delaware, while I was driving Sam McKee would call the races. Needless to say Paul Spears had the heavy favorite, thus I chose to follow him.

As we approached the half I noticed Spears' horse was drifting out. I thought I would hug the rail, thinking he would really bear out in the stretch.

At Delaware, because the speakers are in the infield, a driver can hear every word the announcer says. Going to the ¾'s Sam said, "*Roger will have to back out and come three wide.*"

On the videotape it clearly shows me shaking my head "no". In the stretch Paul's horse did bear out giving me room to come up the inside to win the race by open lengths in 2:01.2.

When Paul got back to the paddock he got a phone call from Bob Steel the Presiding Judge asking if he intentionally bore out to allow me to come up the inside and win.

Spears told the judge, "*Under no uncertain terms would I even let my mother up inside to win a race!*" Up until then Paul Spears never had one infraction, but he got a 3-day suspension that day.

In later years my back started giving me fits so I drove less and less. In 1991 I drove a trotter for my stepson, Troy McDougal, by the name of *Von Prix*.

We were certain we could win the race as we drew the rail. I cut the fractions of 32.2, 1:04.4, 1:35.4 with a final time of 2:06.2.

By the way, at that time if you went a quarter in 33 seconds you would be fined, so as you can see I was pretty good with a stop watch--- or else just damn lucky.

We were expecting to go a mile around 2:00, so when I called Troy after the races and told him how slow we went he told me to give them back the purse money. But of course we didn't.

My last winning drives were with *Florian C* for Tom Noble at Delaware and *Babylon* for Jim Arledge Jr. at The Red Mile.

I have since lost the record for Amateur Drivers at Delaware with 4 out of a 5-year period, but for a while we certainly were on a roll.

As all good drivers say, *"Thanks to the many trainers and owners for giving me a chance to live out a lifelong dream."*

Falcon Seelster and Tom Harmer at The Jug
1985

Dragon's Lair and Jeff Mallet winning
The 1984 Breeders Crown

The Great Nansemond

Wiggle It Jiggleit and Montrell Teague
Winning The Little Brown Jug
2015

CHAPTER ELEVEN

Falcon Seelster, Dragon's Lair, Nansemond & Wiggle It Jiggleit

Over the years I have called many great races such as The Little Brown Jug, The Cane, The Messenger, The Adios, The Provincial Cup, The Monctonian, The Breeders Crown Races and The Hambletonian.

Each one was extremely important to me throughout my sixty-year career; however, I would like to go a bit deeper into four particular races. These races were special to me and also to the many fans that had attended them or continue to talk about them in our beloved sport of Harness Racing.

Some may disagree with me and think there have been better races, but these are my personal standouts. The superstars were horses who for one reason or another are heartfelt to me.

The first I will be talking about is a special horse called **Falcon Seelster**. The *Warm Breeze/ Fashion Trick* colt got his early training in The Maritimes at Brunswick Downs in Moncton, New Brunswick. His trainer was Francis Belliveau who was stabled at a barn located on the final turn of the track at Brunswick Downs. If my memory serves me correctly it was close to the track kitchen, but since I haven't been there since 1991 I may be wrong.

Trainer Tom Harmer purchased *Falcon Seelster* at the beginning of his three-year-old season for $65,000 after he had raced twice in Canada at two.

The new owners were Clara Stable, Charles Day, and Castleton Farms. Over the years I became close friends with Day as he truly felt that *Falcon* could go World Record miles if I was calling the race; more or less because he thought I was Falcons' good luck charm.

As *Falcon* was trained in the Maritimes, his owners did not stake him into The Jug, so Harmer decided to get Jug officials to stage an Open event so he could prove to the world his horse was "As good or better" as those entered in The Jug.

FALCON SEELSTER
September 1985

The day was September 19, 1985. It was a beautiful, warm day at Delaware, Ohio when history would be made in Harness Racing. The grandstands were packed with 47,135 enthusiastic fans that came to watch the great *Nihilator* race in The Little Brown Jug.

Nihilator didn't disappoint, for he won the first division and the final in 1:52.1 with driver William O'Donnell.

O'Donnell also won the other division with *Pershing Square* but then turned the lines over to John Campbell for the final. However, on that day the spotlight before and after The Jug was not on *Nihilator,* but on **Falcon Seelster** who was racing in a $6,000 Invitational Race against five other horses.

That morning I spoke with Harmer about the upcoming race and the fractions he wanted to go to get the World Record, if possible. He predicted 27/55/1:23; but said the final time would be up to *Falcon Seelster*. (At that time *Bret Hanover* held the World Record in the time of 1:53.3)

As a race announcer many will plan ahead on what they will say on the conclusion of a race, but I have never done that. I am spontaneous and play to the moment for there is no guarantee that the race is going to go like you think, and thus can turn into quite a disaster.

I will say that deep in my mind I had always heard from a number of fans that they thought Harness Racing was nowhere near exciting as Thoroughbred Racing. They said they didn't get into the race unless they had made a bet and their horse was winning. Maybe that explains the line that came out during Falcon's race?

The race was early in the card and before The Jug. In the race the five other horses racing against *Falcon Seelster* were *Crown Time Leader, Tequila Star, Skipper Dale Marx, BJ's Reply* and *OB's Falcon Eddie.*

When the gate opened Harmer took *Falcon* to the front. He was cutting the mile with *Falcon* while the other horses stayed in close contention until the ¾'s when Harmer turned his horse loose and opened up.

Elated, I screamed, "**What's the ¾'s gonna be? It's 1:22.4 and Falcon Seelster opens up for Tom Harmer! If you've never been on your feet, you better get up now. It's Falcon Seelster opening up now by 15 lengths, 17, 19. Falcon Seelster and Tom Harmer coming home. Look at the time! 1:51!!!!!!!!**"

That remarkable record stood at Delaware, Ohio for 17 years until a horse named *Million Dollar Cam* with Luc Quelette won The Jug in 2002 with a mile in 1:50.2!

Later that year Charlie Day wanted to go to Capital Raceway in California to break the World Record with *Falcon* and wanted me to call the race.

Needless to say I agreed and so did Dick Fineberg the General Manager as well. A few days before the race Fineberg called Charlie and said, "*We have a problem in that the announcer would not let Roger call the race.*"

Charlie's response, "*Scratch Falcon Seelster.*"

Fineberg pleaded with Day that they had spent a lot of money promoting that race and *Falcon* couldn't scratch out, so they agreed I could call the race on TV from the winner's circle.

As it turned out *Falcon Seelster* failed in his attempt and my friend Charlie Day went to his grave blaming the loss on the fact that Falcon couldn't hear my voice!

But all was not lost for there was a bright spot to that trip as I was to have dinner that night with some regulars at the track. While taking the elevator to the clubhouse, a young lady walked into the elevator and stood with her back to me. I instantly recognized her, leaned close to her ear and sang,

"M-I-C-K-E-Y."

She turned to face me and responded, "M-O-U-S-E."

The lovely woman was no other than actress Annette Funicello of the Mickey Mouse Fame. It just so happened that Annette and her husband, horse trainer Glen Holt, were my dinner partners that evening.

That night I discovered that I was just one month older than my childhood love, Annette.

During the course of dinner I mentioned at The Meadows our racing signal was on satellite and people could purchase an Oak Orion Decoder and watch the races from their home.

Annette purchased a Decoder and she and her husband, Glen, sent 12 horses to race at The Meadows in 1986 and watched them race on satellite.

Although I was disappointed that *Falcon* didn't set a record--- meeting and spending time with Annette was worth the disappointment. She was one classy, beautiful woman who will be remembered by many.

DRAGON'S LAIR

October 1984

The next horse is special to me for he is one of our own that came from The Meadows. His name is **Dragon's Lair**. Dragon was owned by trainer/driver Jeff Mallet, Harvey Heller, and Gary Kornfeld.

Dragon's Lair was a dominant force during his two-year-old season, racing primarily in Pennsylvania. In those days I was involved in a driving career in Amateur Racing.

One day Jeff asked me if I wanted to go a training mile with Dragon. I jumped at the chance! The only problem was I would not be going the mile with the superhorse. I sat behind one of his other top pacers; who is nameless to me today. Nonetheless, it was a great thrill to even be that close to this superstar.

****

It was 1984---the first year of The Breeders Crown. The third event would be held at The Meadows for Two-Year-Old Colt Pacers, featuring the mighty *Nihilator* from The Haughton Stable.

In the early days The Breeders Crown races were held at different tracks rather than the way they are raced at present—all at a single facility.

Leading up to The Breeders Crown at The Meadows, Jay Bergman and myself were the only ones publically supporting *Dragon's Lair*.

I was invited to do a talk show with Spencer Ross in New York City, discussing the chances of *Dragon Lair* pulling an upset. I must admit I am not sure if it was my publicity mind or if I really truly thought it was possible.

During Delaware Week Billy Haughton approached me in The Old Log Cabin and asked if I really thought *Dragon's Lair* was better than *Nihilator*. My response, "Yes!"

Haughton looked at me and said, *"Time will tell."*

The night of the Breeders Crown it was unusually cool and a bit foggy; certainly not what you would call the perfect racing night. The crowd was in excess of 8,000 and ESPN was broadcasting live with Sam Smith, Kenny Rice and Sharon Smith.

Nihilator and William O'Donnell took the First Division in a World Record time of 1:54.3 with *Dragon's Lair* finishing a close second.

The second division was easily won by another Haughton entry, *Pershing Square,* with Billy's son Tommy Haughton in 1:56. Thus, the stage was set for the 2nd Heat Final.

Jeff Mallet and his close friend trainer Mark Goldberg discussed what the strategy should be in the final. They felt that the Haughton team would try to double-team *The Dragon,* so it was essential that Mallet control the race.

They lined up behind the gate from the inside out with *Nihilator, Pershing Square, Dragon's Lair, Broadway Express, Marauder, Witsends Wizard, Warm Breeze* and *Flight of Fire.*

When the gate opened, *Pershing Square* left hard along with *Dragon's Lair* and *Nihilator* got away third. It was quite an early battle going to the quarter when Haughton decided to let Mallet go in the fastest time ever in 26.3!

Mallet had figured they would try to make him take a two-hole trip and he wasn't going to bite. The field in the same order reached the half in 56.3 as Mallet was able to get a soft 2nd quarter in 30 seconds flat.

Down the backside O'Donnell pulled and engaged *Dragon's Lair,* but never could catch up. The third quarter went in 1:25.1---a 28.3 third quarter.

Dragon's Lair dominated to the wire with *Broadway Express* finishing second and a fading *Nihilator* third in a World's Record time of 1:54.1!

Right after the race I was supposed to send the microphone to Kenny Rice but was so thrilled that "The Horse From The Meadows" had won, I tossed the head set and made a beeline to the Winner's Circle. During the trophy celebration Mallet announced that "All his friends were there and a couple of acquaintances."

That night we threw a big party for invited guests at The Holiday Inn, located next to The Meadows. When Billy Haughton and his wife Dottie arrived he came straight to me and said, *"I guess you were right about Dragon's Lair."*

Standing with us was Dick Richardson who trained and drove *Marauder*. I thanked him for racing in The Breeders Crown and he replied, *"I will be back next year and win The Adios."*

He did indeed, defeating *Nihilator* who scratched and declined a third heat, so it was a walkover in 2:27.2 for *Marauder*.

NANSEMOND

If you ask racing fans what their favorite Little Brown Jug was you would most likely get many different answers. Some would pick a year or a winner because of the lightning time the race went—maybe even setting a world record

One of the biggest Jug upsets took place on September 23, 1971 when **Nansemond** upset the powerful *Albatross* in a three-heat battle between *H T Luca, Nansemond* and *Albatross*.

The story of the 1971 Little Brown Jug begins in Detroit, Michigan about a week or so before the Jug. The great *Albatross* had just won a race prepping for The Jug when his driver Stanley Dancer was interviewed.

During the interview Dancer commented, *"All he had to do was jog around the ½ mile track at Delaware to win the Little Brown Jug."* Whether you view this statement as overly confident or cocky, it came back to bite Stanley in the rear!

To this very day it is not known who made copies of the interview, plastering them everywhere at Delaware---even going as far as posting them in the men's room! To say the least, many fans did not appreciate the comment by Dancer; thus they cheered for Herve Filion and *Nansemond* to win the race.

In the first division, *H T Luca* and Del Insko were victorious over *El Patron* and Buddy Gilmour who finished second and *Keystone Journal* and Marc Ferguson finishing third. *Gamely* and Herve finished a disappointing fourth in 1:58.3.

In the second division it was evident what horse the fans wanted to win as they booed Dancer and *Albatross* in the Post Parade. However, the mighty *Albatross* won in 1:58.1 over Herve and *Nansemond* while *Springfield* and Jack Kopas finished third. Rounding out the top four was John Simpson Jr. and *Dexter Hanover*, making the eight horse second heat.

In the second heat the eight horses lined up behind the gate. From the rail out was *Albatross, H T Luca, El Patron, Nansemond, Springfield, Keystone Journal, Dexter Hanover* and *Gamely* on the outside driven by Joe O'Brien.

From the rail *Albatross* hung *Nansemond* to the quarter in 29, with Herve finally taking a seat behind the speedy *Albatross,* while *H T Luca* sat third and *El Patron* fourth, reaching the half in 59.1.

H T Luca and *El Patron* were first up as they got to the ¾'s in 1:29. Around the final turn *H T Luca* tired and *El Patron* went three-wide as Filion and *Nansemond* came to the outside within a ½ length off of *Albatross,* where the two battled. In deep stretch *Nansemond* overtook *Albatross* to win in 1:57.2---equaling the fastest 2nd heat which was set by *Bret Hanover* in 1965.

The horses had earned their post-positions for the third heat by their finish in the 2nd heat. From the inside out were *Nansemond, Albatross,* and *H T Luca* on the outside.

A crowd of 43,460 fans was on their feet for the entire third heat as Herve was determined to be on top and make *Albatross* work for the win and beat him in the stretch if he could.

Herve once told me that he was sure if he got the fractions he wanted, *Nansemond* could out-step *Albatross* coming home.

Needless to say with a quarter in 31.2---the half in 1:03.1 and still able to walk to the three quarters in 1:36.2, *Nansemond* would be hard to beat.

Nansemond stepped home in 28 seconds to easily win The Jug in 2:04.2.

After the race, during the interview Stanley Dancer told the reporters he wouldn't be coming back to race in The Jug until he was sure he could win.

Five years later in 1976 Dancer came back with *Keystone Ore* winning the 2nd division in 1:57 and the 2nd heat in 1:57.2—equaling the World Record for two heats.

It was sort of a grudge match, as *Keystone Ore* had lost to *Armbro Ranger* in The Adios. In The Jug *Armbro Ranger* won the first division in 1:56.4, but finished fifth in the final.

WIGGLE IT JIGGLEIT

As I close out this chapter I saved the next horse for last for in so many ways he and his trainer, driver, and owners have given me some of the biggest thrills of my career.

The horse is none other than **Wiggle It Jiggleit**. Even the name makes me smile. ☺

Wiggle It Jiggleit was victorious in one of the most memorable Little Brown Jugs in the history.

Even the horses' driver, Montrell Teague gets sentimental when he talks about his win that day. The homebred son of *Mr. Wiggles/ Mozzi Hanover* raced alongside *Lost For Words* for nearly 5/8's of a mile, fell behind coming off the last turn, and then rallied in the final strides to win by a nose.

Montrell told Standardbred Canada in an interview, *"I still get emotional every time after watching the replay of that exciting race. It was a super, unreal kind of race. I don't know if any other horse could have done what he did. It's too tough for just a normal horse."*

For the past 51 years I have had the honor to call The Little Brown Jug at Delaware, Ohio, on the third Thursday after Labor Day. I can't imagine a more thrilling, hard fought battle with a horse that appeared to be losing, only to come back in the final two strides to win The Jug.

In his two heats *Wiggle It Jiggleit* only saw the pylons for 3/8's of a mile: the opening 1/4 of the second division and the first 1/8th of the final heat.

The weather on September 24, 2015 (which by the way is the latest date the Jug can be held since the all-weather track was installed at Delaware) was ideal for horseracing with sunny skies and temperatures ranging from 75-80 degrees.

The Jug had drawn a field of 15 Three-Year-Old Pacers, which would go in two eliminations and a final. The first four finishers in each division would return for the 2nd heat final. The purse that day was a record of $677,000.

Wiggle It Jiggleit, by *Mr. Wiggles* out of *Mozzi Hanover* by *Jenna's Beach Boy*, came into The Jug with 17 wins for the year and was the favorite to win over hometown favorite *Lost For Words*, trained by Brian Brown and driven by David Miller.

Wiggle It Jiggleit drew post 5 in the second division while *Lost For Words* headed the opening division from post 1.

In the first division David Miller went right to the top and controlled the field with fractions of 27, 55.3 and 1:23.1.

He was challenged coming home by *Yankee Bounty* and Yannick Gingras, but could only come within 1½ lengths at the wire in 1:50.2.

Rockin In Heaven with Trevor Henry was third and *Split The House* driven by Tim Tetrick finished fourth, thus qualifying for the final.

In the second division *Artspeak* and Scott Zeron went right to the top in a speedy 26.3 with *My Hero Ron* taking a seat for Yannick Gingras.

Montrell Teague and *Wiggle It Jiggleit* were moving, coming to the half after the leader *Artspeak* in 54.3. Montrell and *Wiggle* were hung from there to the ¾'s in 1:21---a 26.2 third quarter.

Montrell and *Wiggle It Jiggleit* showed he was the one to beat by drawing away in 1:49.2 by a margin of 1¼ lengths beating out *Artspeak*.

Arque Hanover and Corey Callahan closed from sixth to be beaten by 2 lengths.

In the final the horses lined up behind the gate from the inside out with *Wiggle It Jiggleit, Lost For Words, Artspeak, Yankee Bounty, Rockin In Heaven, My Hero Ron* and *Arque Hanover*. The horse *Split The House* was a Judges scratch.

The opening 1/4 was a bit rocky for *Wiggle It Jiggleit* who made a few skips going to the 1/8. Meanwhile, *Lost For Words* went to the top in 27 flat with *My Hero Ron* sitting second. *Montrell Teague* felt it safer for his horse *Wiggle It* to sit on the outside---and that they did for the rest of the mile.

Wiggle It Jiggleit was parked to the ½ before getting to the top in 54.1. *Lost For Words* never gave up and the two fought head-to-head, toe-to-toe and stride-for-stride down the backside as the battle turned into a raging war!

The two rivals reached the ¾'s in 1:21.1 with *Wiggle It* edging a nose in front. But around the final turn David Miller and *Lost For Words* took over and opened up by a length and a quarter. Coming off the final turn it appeared Miller and his horse was home free.

All of a sudden in the stretch the margin started to shrink to a length--- a half--- a neck--- and finally in the final two strides, *Wiggleit Jiggleit* wins by a neck in 1:49.3.

After the race Sam McKee announced on TV, *"I do not believe what I just saw!"* I turned the microphone back on and replied, *"It's a shame there has to be a loser, but that's the way it is in horseracing. But Lost For Words is no loser, folks. He just got beat today!"*

The owner of *Wiggle It Jiggleit*, George Teague is quoted saying, *"I thought we were beat at the top of the stretch and I couldn't watch."*

Wiggle's trainer, Clyde Francis, basically said the same thing; and driver Montrell said he was so into the race he forgot to pop the earplugs!

With that win *Wiggle It Jiggleit* became the 8th gelding to win The Jug, the first supplemental entry to win, and Montrell was the 2nd youngest driver to win The Jug at age 24.

That year *Wiggle It Jiggleit* was named, *"The Horse of the Year"* by The USHWA.

There's no question that these 4 races written in this chapter have special meaning to me----but in different ways.

The "Most Remembered" would be **Falcon Seelster**; "The Biggest Upset" is **Nansemond**; "The Most Gratifying" is **Dragon's Lair**, and last but not least, "The Best Race" goes to **Wiggle It Jiggleit.**

Derek Delaney at the Vincent Delaney Memorial in Ireland

Driving a horse in the Irish Sea

Alexis Laidler
The Leading Trainer for 10 straight years in GB, Wales,
Scotland and Ireland

Mike Wilder at Portmarnock Raceway
2018

Aaron Merriman at Portmarnock Raceway
2016

© Copyright www.Ironia-Art.com

George Brennan at Portmarnock
2015

Driving a pair of trotters down the streets of Dublin

Steve Wolf, Nadina Ironia and myself at Portmarnock
2015

Planting a Memorial Tree for Vincent Delaney
Oakwood Stud near Dublin, Ireland
2014

Dan Noble at Portmarnock
2017

Wally Hennessey at Portmarnock
2014

Alexis Laidler and Roger

CHAPTER TWELVE

The International Races

A part of my life that has been so fulfilling is my International
Travel to call races. I do believe this is due to my calling The Little Brown Jug for so many years.

Since 1980 I have been blessed to call races in Canada (19 tracks) Sweden (2) Norway (1) Finland (2) Australia (1) Wales (1) and Ireland (1).

Just when I think my International Travel days are over we get an offer to call races at yet another track. After 60 years in the business, I still don't know how to say 'no.'

****

In 1980 I went to Canada when I was invited to call races at Barrie Raceway by Al Josey. This started things internationally for me.

Those were the days I could still fit into my Steady Star Sports Jacket. We did a TV feature sitting on the window ledge of the announcers' booth while calling a race. (I was also a bit more daring and coordinated in those days.)

Later that year we were invited to call races at Elmira and Kingston Park. In the years to follow there were trips to Flamboro and Frederickton, when the great Buddy Gilmour who drove in the races missed his flight coming home.

We were asked to come to New Brunswick Downs in 1991 to call The Monctonian. Later that year we went to the Western Fair for a Drivers Championship and Windsor for The Provincial Cup. Trips in later years were to Exhibition Park, Queensbury Downs and Charlottetown for The Gold Cup and Saucer in 2000.

On the trip to Charlottetown it was arranged I was to call The Gold Cup and Saucer, but when I was speaking to *Vance Cameron* the announcer I quickly realized that nobody had spoken to him about it.

Whenever I am asked to call races at different tracks I always make sure that the announcer there OK's it, so I went to the officials and graciously declined to call the race knowing how much calling the race meant to Vance.

After speaking with the officials it was arranged I would announce races Friday and Saturday from the old infield Judges Stand with a wireless microphone. To this day I don't think Vance knows the rest of the story about that trip. Needless to say, it was a great experience.

The travels continued with tracks at Truro and Clinton for Legends Day in 2011. That was a thrill of a lifetime. (Note the photo cover is from Clinton)

Randy Pullen from Sarnia contacted me about making a tour of Ontario Racetracks in 2016. That year we announced at Hiawatha Horse Park and Leamington Raceway. In 2017 we announced at Mohawk, Dresden and Leamington; and in 2018 we were at Grand River, Hanover and Leamington for a third straight year.

My first trip to Europe was in 1993 when we announced at Ostersunds Travet and Axevalla in Sweden. The problem we had with that trip was the Pittsburgh Penquins were in The Stanley Cup that year and the games were live from Sweden from 2 a.m. till 5 a.m. (While in Axevalla I drove in an amateur event—finishing fourth in a field of 10.)

The Swedes are big partiers and we partied well past midnight. We had a great time but had to get up early to travel the next morning. Also, that time of year was daylight 24 hours a day.

In 1996 I made my first of five straight years calling The Oslo Grand Prix in Norway. The invitation was extended by Race Secretary Arnlioth Heltberg, which I readily accepted.

In the foreign trips the pronunciation of names is the same but they are not familiar with the added sayings such as, "Passing the Stands," or "Down the Backside."

We were well received and had a great time every year. One memory from the trip--- and it wasn't racing related--- was when they took those involved in the race from Canada, New Zealand, and others on a trip to Holmenkollbakken where the ski jump for the 1952 Olympics was held. For those who remember The Wide World of Sports on ABC—their opening for years was The Thrill of Victory and The Agony of Defeat.

One night we were taken to dinner at one of the finest restaurants, The Rivers Edge, and had a tremendous meal of every type of seafood. The only problem was that driver *Trevor Richie* didn't like seafood, so he and his wife ate at a Steak House down the road.

The unusual part of racing there is that I called the races from the fourth floor on a tower past the finish line. Also, the Judges would interrupt the call over the PA system when a horse was disqualified for breaking.

Another great site was whenever a horse won from Sweden they paraded around the track carrying the Swedish flag. When they approached the Swedish fans the women------ and I mean the majority of the beautiful blondes---- would stand up and wave Swedish flags while being topless! Now that was a site for sore and tired eyes!

Some of the winners I had the pleasure to call were *Ina Scott, Zoogin, Huxable Hornline, Ganymeade* and *Victory Tilly.*

*****

In 1997 I was invited to Australia for The Inter Dominion Pacing Championship at Adelaide's Globe Derby Park. We visited a number of tracks in Australia, but were only permitted to call the co-feature the night of the final. That turned out to be one of my most memorable calls-- at least in Australia.

Those days I always had a saying of *"a horse being nailed to the rail."* I just picked the wrong horse to use it with for the name of the horse was *'Messiah.'* (The call can be heard on You Tube)

In 1998 the Managing Director of Vermo Racetrack in Helsinki, Finland, Jorma Ojapelto, contacted me. They were going to have an evening of American Style racing and wanted me to call the races.

The outriders were dressed as Cowboys and Indians and the food was American fare---serving hot dogs, hamburgers and French fries.

The racing was great and I was invited back the next year to announce at Vermo and another track called Jokimaa Lahti.

In 2009 Huw Evans of Tregaron, Wales asked me if I would be available to call two days of racing at Tregaron on the grass course, as they were going for a World's Record on a ½ mile track of grass.

It was the most beautiful setting for racing and by far the greenest grass I have ever seen.

After each race the track crew would roll the track to pack it down as to prevent slippage of the race bikes.

During that trip I was fortunate to meet Alexis Laidler, the trainer who has the most wins in England, Wales, Scotland and Ireland. (See page 189)

Alexis was just starting her run with top honors and it has continued for 10 or 11 straight years. This beautiful young woman could win any contest for the best dressed. She dresses to the hilt in mini-skirts and leather knee-high boots. Her husband, Rocker (Yes, that's really his name) is a top driver as well.

Alexis has also won many under saddle events with pacers. By the way, she did break the World's Record.

****

This important chapter of my life all started when I got a call one day from a friend of mine in Florida.

In 2014 Steve Wolf of Harness Link contacted me with "*Have I got a gig for you!*" The gig was to announce The Vincent Delaney Memorial at Portmarnock in Dublin, Ireland.

It's a two-day affair and the main race is for Two-Year-Old Pacers called The Vincent Delaney Memorial. (In my opinion this would be a well-suited race for Roger Hammer)

They hold eliminations on Saturday with the final on Sunday. They have since added a filly division with the same format.

The prestigious race was named after Vincent Delaney who passed away at the early age of 27. His two brothers, Derek and James, wanted to memorialize their brother with a Harness Race in his memory, thus The Vincent Delaney Memorial was born.

When I heard the story it touched me so much I dropped several important dates I had in The States to make way for the trip to Ireland. It has grown each and every year with more than 200 visitors who come from around the world, including numerous American Sponsors.

The Delaney Brothers own Oakwood Stud where they stand *Foreclosure N*---one of the top-pacing stallions in Ireland.

Foreclosure N was campaigned in The States by trainer Ron Burke.

Oakwood Stud is located about an hours drive from Dublin. While there we make a regular trip to the farm where they have a Memorial Garden that is positioned in the middle of their ½ mile-training track.

We even participated in the planting of a tree in 2014, which is getting quite large. The Memorial also has a large Granite Marker for each year with inscribed names of any new visitors. (See page 195)

In the years I have traveled to Ireland, I have been accompanied by top drivers Wally Hennessey, George Brennan, Aaron Merriman, Dan Noble and last year Mike Wilder.

Jody Jamison and Dexter Dunn are drivers who came and drove there from Canada and New Zealand. All have said the trip is a must for any Harness Racing fan.

Harness horsemen in Ireland really are the greatest because they truly enjoy what they are doing. It is a family operation and they love winning, as we all do.

However, the monetary gain makes it mighty tough as purses are quite low and at times only the first two or three finishers get a piece of the purse.

The expense of operation is high, as most have to ship to Ireland by ferry from Scotland, which is very costly and the racing is very competitive.

****

I must relate a story about our own Aaron Merriman.

When he went there to race in 2016 he had no winners on the Saturday card and if you are familiar with Aaron this is a rarity.

One of the Irish horsemen approached him after the races and said, *"I watch you every program at The Meadows and you are very aggressive. You better get more aggressive here."*

Aaron listened to him and won a few races the following day, on Sundays card.

Another thing I'd like to mention is the interaction with the fans; especially the youngsters who are fascinated with the drivers. The time Dan Noble and Mike Wilder went there to drive they were swarmed with the young, enthusiastic fans.

Wilder even brought over driving gloves from Big D's Tack to pass out to the youngsters they met. It was a wonderful well-received gesture that I'm sure they will forever cherish.

In 2018 American television journalist, Heather Vitale, arranged a trip to the Irish Sea for Mike Wilder and I to jog horses trained by Sean Kane at Bettystown Beach and in the sea. (See page 188)

What an experience and by far one of our most enjoyable times in Ireland. It was right up there with the time I got to drive a horse drawn carriage ride on the streets of Dublin. (See page 193)

We do this every other year and I have had the pleasure of driving Fresian Trotters with cars to my right and people on the sidewalks on my left.

On one occasion I went inside a pylon (actually the curb) but no harm, no foul.

For the V.D.M. Weekend they even have a "Best Dressed" contest for the women and men alike, just like they do at The Kentucky Derby. It is quite a pleasure to see folks attending the races in their finery.

Youngsters wear a set of colors—just like their fathers or mothers who are drivers.

Winners' circle is always filled with 15 to 50 people. All the action is caught by one of the worlds' best photographers', Nadina Ironia. Her beautiful works can be found on Facebook or her website.

In closing this chapter, I am so looking forward to once again go to Vincent Delaney Memorial Weekend in Ireland this year in 2019. (Hopefully to have a book signing there.)

Also, I'm looking forward to my annual trip at Ontario, Canada. The Good Lord Willing and the Creek Don't Rise...... BE THERE!

CHAPTER THIRTEEN

Pittsburgh Sports Announcing

When I came to The Meadows in 1976 I knew that Pittsburgh was a big sports town with die-hard loyal fans but I never dreamed I would be a big part of it.

That year The University of Pittsburgh got off to a 2-0 start. On Wednesday the 22nd of September, Dean Billick, The Sports Information Director was in the Clubhouse at The Meadows.

The next morning Dean contacted me and asked if I had ever done PA work for Football and Basketball before. The answer of course was "yes," for in the late 50s and 60s I had done both play-by-play and P.A. announcing in Xenia and at Wilmington College.

Dean told me he thought Pitt had a good chance of becoming The National Champion as they were rated #3 in the country. Billick said he wanted to liven up Pitt Stadium and thought I was the man who could do it.

Since the games were on Saturday afternoon (at that time the Meadows raced Saturday nights) the answer was a definite yes. Thus I had a great 7-year run at Pitt from 1976 through 1983.

When television eventually took over and dates were changed from afternoon to evening (sometimes a Thursday or Friday night game on top of me calling races at The Meadows) I regretfully had to give up working at Pitt.

My first game was September the 25th. Pitt easily beat Temple in front of 34,000 enthusiastic fans. Man, that was like a Little Brown Jug crowd!

That year Pitt was undefeated and went on to win the National Championship with an incredible 12-0 Record.

The first game of the season Quarterback Robert Haygood broke his leg and young Matt Cavanaugh took over. Of course he was backed up by the likes of Tony Dorsett, Elliott Walker, Gordon Jones, Jim Corbett, Randy Hollaway, Al Romano and Jim Cramer.

I loved to play with the players' names on the P.A. by over-emphasizing them to get the crowds reaction; and it worked for it was well received by the fans.

A young defensive player came along with a rather ordinary name but was far from ordinary on the field. There was no name to really play with that year, but I recalled the great Boog Powell in baseball and how the fans would chant "Boog" so I thought to myself *"Why not Hugh?"*

Number 99 was Hugh Green---- a three-time All American at Pitt from 1978 through 1980. In time I would say, *"Tackle made by #99,"* and the crowd would yell, *"Hugh"* and I would say, *"Green."*

One of my proudest moments was when Green was named 'Dapper Dan Athlete of the Year' in his senior year. As he received his award, the crowd harmoniously chanted, *"Hugh, Hugh, Hugh."*

*****

I don't want to slight the great Dan Marino, one of the all-time greatest to ever come out of the Burgh. In 1976 Johnny Majors was Head Coach when he retired and was replaced by Jackie Sherrill.

I only had one problem dealing with a coach (who shall remain nameless) sending me a note telling me to stop making individual stars of his players, for they were a team.

My reply was *"If you would pay more attention to the game rather than the P.A. system, you might win more games."* Then I stamped the note with a pad that read, *"BULL SHIT."*

Basketball was fun and there were many stories with such greats as Sam Clancy, Carlton Neverson, Larry Harris, David Olinger, J. R. Ryan and Sammie Ellis to name a few.

The one story I like to tell is the one about Rollie Massimino, the coach of Villanova who would throw little tantrums when something wasn't going right on the floor.

I was usually sitting very close to the opponents coach when one time he went into one of his jumping up and down fits, turned and faced me as he smiled and said, *"Did I go overboard on that one?"*

*****

By the way, it was at The Fieldhouse when I first saw Jerry Erenstein who years later would become my good friend and co-host on The Meadows Racing Network.

I heard this awful racket near the end of a game and went to see what the ruckus was. It was Jerry screaming at the referees near the exit doors.

Several years later it was Dejavu' when I spotted him doing the same thing to some of the drivers at The Meadows.

I am running out of space in this book so the last two instances will be brief.

I was asked to be the P.A. announcer for The Pittsburgh Maulers in 1984 for their one-year season in The U.S. Football League.

I also served as P.A. Announcer for the Indoor Football Gladiators of The Arena Football League in 1987 and 1988. It was yours truly who came up with the phrase, *"The War on the Floor."*

Announcing for Pitt and other Pennsylvania teams was an honor and very special to me. As I said, our great city of Pittsburgh has some of the best, loyal fans in the country and I am glad to be a part of it.

Heather Wilder
USHWA Dan Patch Banquet
2016

Richard Stillings and Dave Palone
2018 Hall of Fame Trot
Goshen, New York

Brian Sears
Hall of Fame
Goshen 2016

Jimmy Takter, RonWaples, Dave Palone, Dick Stillings, Brian Sears, Wally Hennessey and DavidMiller
Hall of Fame Trot 2018

The Great Nevele Pride

David Miller at the Dan Patch Dinner
Las Vegas 2013

Sarah Wertz My # 1 Fan
The Little Brown Jug

Actor Jimmy Stewart at Matinee Race Program
Indiana, Pa. on his 75th Birthday
1983

Beth, Brian, Julia and Tommy Larouere

Curby Stillings, Tracy Bittner, Kerri Charlino, Vicki Howard,
Me, Nevele and Joey Porco
Pompano Park
2001

CHAPTER FOURTEEN

Special People and Places

In this chapter I will list in order (from the beginning to the present time) a little something about each person who has positively affected my life in one way or another.

There will be short comments on what these people did for me throughout the years. Also, at the end of the chapter I would like to share three very important times that will forever be special to me: When I was asked to say the eulogy at funerals of very dear friends of mine.

*****

My parents Cecil and Irene—My parents who allowed me to live the life I always wanted and dreamed of having. They supported me 100% and did their best to steer me down the right path of life's journey.

Don Huston--- My Uncle who took me under his wing and taught me what needed to be done along the way. He was instrumental in getting me started both in broadcasting and racing.

Phil Mauger --- The man who asked me to fill in for him at The Red Mile, The Knox County Fair in Mount Vernon, and The Ohio State Fair. Later he was my Assistant Announcer at Delaware.

Richard Wilson --- The General Manager of Pompano Park who came to The Greene County Fair in Xenia and heard me call a race of 12 trotters (which 11 made breaks) but still had the faith to hire me to announce races at Pompano Park: The Winter Capital of Harness Racing.

William Van Buren—The man who got me the full-time job at The Red Mile from 1967 through 1975, in both Spring and Fall meets.

Delvin Miller, John Townsend, Ed Ryan, and **Joe Hardy** ---- Four great men who hired me in 1976 to announce races at The Meadows; thus starting my lifelong career there. And to all the owners over the years that supported me and kept me on through present day.

Corwin Nixon ---- The man who recommended me to Hank Thomson when Charlie Hinkle left his job at The Jug to move to California.

Tom Thomson ---- Who became the brother I never had; and to the entire Thomson Family who accepted me as part of their family for the past six generations.

Phil Terry ---- I first met Phil when he was Chief of Security at Delaware then became Marketing Manager. He was also at one time Fair Manager for The Delaware County Fair.

To all the people I have worked with over the years at The Red Mile, Pompano Park Racetrack and The Meadows. You have all been very special to me.

To every Speed Superintendent at The County and State Fairs I have worked with from 1960 to the present.

Steve Wolf ---- Thank you for arranging me to meet Derek Delaney. Derek has given me the opportunity to call the biggest weekend in Irish Racing at Portmarnock Raceway in Dublin, Ireland for The Vincent Delaney Memorial.

Randy Pullen ---- The person for the past three years who has went to great detail in arranging trips to Ontario tracks each year.

To all the people that invited me back to make special appearances at various tracks that were important to me in my early years of announcing.

The Owners, Trainers, Drivers and Caretakers who do all the hard work putting on the show that I so much enjoy announcing. I truly mean it when I say I haven't worked a day in my life, for that is the case if you truly love what you are doing.

To the millions of Harness Racing Fans all over the world-- I want to thank you for accepting me and allowing me to become part of your life as well. I always look forward to meeting one and all, each year I return.

Finally, to my family both past ---- **Norma & Cami Sue**, and present---- **Barb, Troy, Tyler, Nevele, Robin, Colton, Dustin, Regan** and **Kinsley**. Thank you so much for putting up with me over the years as I truly realize how hard it has been for you with my being away so much and missing special events in your lives. But you can be assured that you are always in my thoughts, day in and day out. I love you all.

*****

The hardest thing I have had to do in life has been to say a eulogy at the funerals for three of my dearest friends.

The first one was for **Mary Lib Miller** (the wife of Delvin Miller) in the old school house at Meadowcroft Village. Thankfully it was very easy and I am sure I said just what Mary Lib would have wanted me to say.

The next was for **Chip Noble**. Chip was a great trainer and driver of many good horses. His wife, Deb, called and asked me if I would do the eulogy. At first I told her I couldn't, then I changed my mind and said I would, almost in the same breath.

I had known the Noble family for so many years: in fact for five generations. The night before the funeral I was up most of the night writing and going over it word by word, as I wanted it to be perfect. I hope it was, for the families' sake.

And then there was my dear friend, **Sam McKee**, who had meant so much to me from the young age of six when he nominated me for Horseman of the Year. I'm so thankful to Richard Hackett of The Horseman and Fair World for introducing us.

After I wrote Sam's eulogy I made the trip to New Jersey with Phil Terry. Phil told me he could have delivered it by the time we arrived there as I had gone over it time and time again.

I am a very sentimental and emotional person and am able to cry at the drop of a hat and the only way you are able to do these things is to practice it over and over. Maybe this section doesn't belong in this book, but it is a very important part of my life and who I am.

My family
Nevele, Dustin, Regan and Kinsley

Dustin, Nevele, Kinsley and Regan

Presentation with Nevele
2001

Colton, Troy, Robin and Tyler McDougal

Uncle Don & Aunt Carol

2016

My granddaughters, Kinsley and Regan
The Meadows 2017

Carl Becker, Kurt Becker and Steve Cross
Carl's Induction into The Communicators Hall of Fame
2018

My granddaughters, Kinsley and Regan

My granddaughter Kinsley's Baptism

Heather Wilder at Delaware
2016

CHAPTER FIFTEEN

My Life Today

I would be lying if I said my life today is as easy as ever because the fact of the matter is I am now 76 years old and still trying to do what I did when I was 40.

My schedule has not changed much in the last five years, except with the addition of the tracks in Ontario, the trip to Ireland, and various guest appearances.

The regular schedule of 195 days at The Meadows with 30 vacation days to make the trips all over the world keeps me pretty busy.

At The Meadows we race primarily Monday, Tuesday, Wednesday and Friday afternoons, with a few variations during the year.

As far as fairs, I currently have 5 in Pennsylvania, 4 in Ohio (including Jug Week) 1 in West Virginia, 2 in Virginia and a trip to McGhees' Mile in Aiken, South Carolina.

I will once again go to Ireland for the Vincent Delaney Memorial Weekend and hopefully our 3-track tour in Ontario.

At that pace we should easily reach the 180,000th race call shortly after The Jug. There also may be some special appearances made if anything else comes up.

I went into last year, (2018) not knowing I would be going to Fryeburg, Maine and Plainridge Park, along with returns to Urbana and Greenville, Ohio.

On a daily basis I usually arrive at The Race Office around 8:30 in the morning, seven days a week, no matter if we have a live racing card or not. When I'm in town I always stop in the office Sunday morning before going to Chapel with Pastor Joe. To me, it is a much easier routine if you do it on a daily basis.

Even if I'm out of town on Saturday, I always try to get back for Chapel services.

I try to make it to my daughter Nevele and her husband, Dustin's home a couple nights a week to spend quality time with my two precious granddaughters, Regan and Kinsley.

I also have what I refer to as 'two adopted' daughters. One is Beth Larouere, who was my cardiac rehab nurse in 2001. I usually try to go to dinner with Beth and her husband, Brian, and their children, Tommy and Julia.

Their son Tommy is playing Middle school hockey so I try to make a few of his games.

My other 'adopted' daughter is Heather Wilder. Heather is the daughter of Danny and Ruth Altmeyer, and the wife of driver Mike Wilder. Heather works with me every year at Delaware and The Dan Patch Awards. Mike and Heather have two beautiful teenage daughters named Scarlett and Lauren.

It's hard to go to dinner on a regular basis with the Wilder's, due to their busy schedule, but I try to see them at least once a month.

As far as hobbies go I really don't have any, except I am a news junkie and love any movie with a Clint Eastwood connection. I must admit I was not a big fan of his spaghetti westerns in the early days, but absolutely loved Million Dollar Baby, Sully, and Absolute Power.

I've tried golf for many of the drivers and trainers play golf so it would be nice to hang out with them when we aren't racing, but with my back problems I had to stop.

In the earlier days I did play 18 holes at Pompano Park with Sandra Palmer who won 19 LPGA Tour events when Pompano Park had their Par Three Golf Course. I also beat Jerry Erenstein one time at Seven Springs in Pennsylvania.

I've had what is known as a Keyhole-Bi-Pass and Left Knee Replacement. The unusual thing was that I put both off until after The Little Brown Jugs in 2000 and 2003.

After the heart surgery I only missed three days of announcing and a week after knee surgery.

Quinton Patterson the Grandstand Maintenance and Mr. Do Everything at The Meadows, accompanied me to the announcers' booth and then to my car every night for a few weeks.

****

What does the future hold for me? Only The Good Lord will determine that and I'll have to take one day at a time. But I'm grateful for the life I've been given and the people I've met.

I feel like I'm the luckiest man alive for I have the best job in the world and the greatest family and friends.

I hope you enjoyed reading this book and know that I appreciate each and every one of you.

By the grace of God after 76 wonderful years, I'm still here calling races and hope to continue doing so as long as I can to entertain all of you. I hope you can and will always....

"BE THERE"

In conclusion to the story of "BE THERE", it was in 1976 when I came to The Meadows. A man by the name of Aubry Lee was the advertising executive. We were recording a one-minute radio commercial for the week and it came up short. We thought and thought and couldn't come up with any other add-ons to fill the time, then it hit me and I said, *"I GOT IT!"* On the next recording I added *"Be There*!" and that is how the saying came to be.

Roger

CHAPTER SIXTEEN

P.S.

After the book was completed and the final touches were made such as putting all the correct page numbers in the index, three very important stories surfaced that I had overlooked.

Without having to re-write the lengthy index we decided to put in a P.S. Chapter for this book couldn't be printed without these three stories.

****

The first took place during my freshman year at Wilmington College. At the time I was Manager and Scorekeeper for the men's Basketball team. One of my duties was to lock the dressing room when the team had gone up to the court for the game.

We had travelled to Kentucky to take on Berea. Coach Fred Raizk had given his final pep talk to the players then went to the men's room. Thinking that everyone had left the dressing room I locked the door and joined the team on the court.

The National Anthem had played and the starting line-ups were announced when a young lad of maybe 12 years old came running to the scorer's table, saying that there was someone in the dressing room who had been locked in and was screaming to be let out.

I immediately gave the key to one of the players who went to the dressing room. Minutes later, Coach Raizk appeared on the court, white as snow. If looks could kill I would not be here to tell the story.

Coach was so upset he didn't talk to me for days; however, several weeks later, Clipping Service started pouring in from all over the world.

Nearly 200 newspapers—some from Europe and Australia---had picked up the story with the headline, *"Who Needs The Coach?"*

****

The second occurred at Pompano Park during The Quarter Horse Meet in the 70's. There was a horse named Bull Sit that I had to call so as not to be mistaken for anything similar. I had no problem with Bull Sit but one night he got into a race with another horse and for the only time in more than 178,000 calls I didn't finish a race call. What do you say after saying it is Bull Sit on top and Scoop It Up is second?

****

The third story was at The Meadows with a horse named Mr Rogers. As they were going to the half I called it is Mr Rogers chasing Hot Panties. The last half of the race I tried to announce as usual but I kept laughing most of the time.

The Announcers Booth
Clinton County Fair
2015

About the Author

Victoria Howard is a published author of 18 books. She has appeared on Fox & Friends, Good Day L.A. and Good Morning Sacramento. Several of her books have been written up in The New York Times, The Huffington Post, The Pittsburgh Press and The Miami Herald.

Several equine books Howard wrote are *Meadow Skipper, Murray Brown, Roosevelt Raceway, Rose Runners* and the children's book, *Max and Molly: A Horse Love Story.*

Her book *The Kentucky Horse Park: Paradise Found* was the Winnie Winner at the NYC Equus Film Festival in 2017.

Victoria also pens a bi-monthly column in Harness Racing Update called SUPERSTAR FEMALES OF HARNESS RACING, honoring the many women in the sport.

She is a horse lover who has bred, owned and raced Standardbreds for 40 years and currently co-owns 18 horses who she calls her children.

In 2011 Victoria was named VIP Who's Who Woman of the Year Worldwide.

Ms. Howard lives in Florida with her dog, Max.

Index